Millicent Garrett Fawcett

Tales in political economy

Millicent Garrett Fawcett

Tales in political economy

ISBN/EAN: 9783742802958

Manufactured in Europe, USA, Canada, Australia, Japa

Cover: Foto ©Andreas Hilbeck / pixelio.de

Manufactured and distributed by brebook publishing software (www.brebook.com)

Millicent Garrett Fawcett

Tales in political economy

TALES

IN

POLITICAL ECONOMY.

TALES

IN

POLITICAL ECONOMY.

BY

MILLICENT GARRETT FAWCETT,
AUTHOR OF "POLITICAL ECONOMY FOR BEGINNERS," &c.

London:
MACMILLAN AND CO.
1874.

[*The Right of Translation and Reproduction is Reserved.*]

LONDON:
R. CLAY, SONS, AND TAYLOR, PRINTERS,
BREAD STREET HILL.

PREFACE.

IT is hoped that these little tales may be of some use to those who are trying to teach Political Economy. I cannot let them go to press without a word of apology to Miss Martineau for my plagiarism of the idea, which she made so popular thirty years ago, of hiding the powder, Political Economy, in the raspberry jam of a story.

Oct. 1874.

CONTENTS.

	PAGE
I.—THE SRIMATS,	1
II.—THE SHIPWRECKED SAILORS,	14
III.—ISLE PLEASANT,	52
IV.—THE ISLANDERS' EXPERIENCE OF FOREIGN TRADE,	79

TALES IN POLITICAL ECONOMY.

I.

The Srimats.

Free trade—Protection of native industry.

I WAS spending a week in a country house a short time ago in which there was also staying an old sailor, Captain Adam. He told me some wonderful stories of adventures he had had when he was young; and it occurred to me that some of them might teach people a good deal about political economy, if they would take the trouble to use their heads a little. The first story that he told me I shall call a free-trade story, because I think it gives a very good example of what people gain by free trade, and shows also how it is that some people are injured through the introduction of free trade.

Captain Adam was once cruising in the Indian ocean to the west of the island of Sumatra. His object was to land on a small island inhabited by the descendants of some of the first Dutch settlers in Sumatra, and to set up a communication between them and Acheen for trading purposes. The most remarkable thing about the people who inhabited this island was that they had had no intercourse with any other people for two hundred years. They were not dependent on any other nation for food, clothing, or machinery; everything that they used they made themselves; they had no trade either with Europe or with the other islands of the archipelago. So far as getting any good from mixing or trading with other people was concerned, they might as well have lived in the moon.

Captain Adam found the Srimats, as they were called, much more civilized than he had expected. They were mild, gentle, and very courteous to strangers; they lived in houses neatly and carefully built; they were completely and simply dressed; they spoke a kind of *patois* of Dutch and Malay, in which Dutch took the chief part: and they had an organized system of government, which the whole tribe regarded with great pride and veneration. This government was very curious. It consisted of a kind of council or parliament, which possessed absolute power over the life and property of every member of the tribe. There was nothing so very strange in this; but the thing that astonished Captain Adam was that no one but the hereditary members of this council was allowed to own the palm trees which yielded the palm oil; and in order to make their monopoly the more valuable, the council had ordained that no Srimat should allow the light of the sun to enter his dwelling. There was not a window to be seen throughout the place. The doors were hung with heavy double matting, through which not a chink of light could pass. The Srimats would certainly have died of suffocation had they not been graciously permitted by their chiefs to take down the matting at night, and thus let some fresh air into the darkened cells in which they were condemned to live.

The object of the council in making this extraordinary rule, was to secure a good market for their palm oil, by making it necessary that it should be burnt all through the day. If they had heard as much about free trade as we have in England, they would have been able to prove most effectually that to exclude the light of the sun from Srimat dwellings was simply to protect native industry. The council owned the palm trees; palm oil was made, by their rule about the windows, a first necessary of life. Two-thirds of the Srimats found their constant occupation in tending the trees and preparing the oil. In return for the oil which they necessarily consumed, the Srimats gave to their chiefs the best of everything that they possessed. The oil sometimes ran short; then what competition and strife there was among the different families of the tribe to see which could give the most costly presents to the chiefs in exchange for the sacred oil.

Captain Adam soon found that the question of the oil stood in the way of his being able to effect his object of setting up a communication for the exchange of merchandize and agricultural produce between the Srimats and the rest of the world. One of the old chiefs, to whom he broached the subject, pointed out, with much gravity, that his project was impracticable. "Two-thirds of our people," he said, "are occupied in our most important industry, the making of palm oil; the other third work hard to provide enough food and raiment for us all. We can only just produce enough to maintain the tribe in decency and comfort; we have no surplus that we could exchange for the products of other lands."

"Your soil must be very fertile," replied Captain Adam, "and your people very industrious and very skilful workmen if one-third of the tribe is able to produce all that is required by the whole Srimat population."

"Yes, yes; it is true," said the old man. "We have much to be thankful for." And he gazed upwards to the bad-smelling palm-oil lamp, the emblem to him of all that was sacred.

"I have been thinking," said the Captain, "that you have much more to be thankful for than you know of. Two-thirds of your people spend their lives in manufacturing this oil. Give me leave to put out all the lamps, and let my men knock holes in the walls of every house in the place; and you will have two-thirds of your people free to turn to the cultivation of spices, rice, and coffee, which you could send away, and receive in return agricultural implements, English cutlery, calico, and other things which you never will be able to make, but which we in England can make any quantity of."

The old chief frowned, and said very sternly, "Knock holes in the walls of our houses! Allow the sun to flood our market with his light! Our island would be ruined: our most important industry would be destroyed in a day. We should have 400 people, who now work in the palm plantations and in the oil presses, reduced to beggary at one blow!"

"But consider for one moment," urged Captain

Adam: "these 400 people work hard all their lives to produce a light very inferior to that which you could all get for nothing if only you would have windows."

"The government is entrusted to the owners of the palm plantations," said the chief. "Put yourself in our place, and tell me if you would throw 400 people out of employment for the sake of a sentimental preference for the light of the sun over the light of the oil lamps. Call our people together. Describe your scheme of knocking holes in their walls and abandoning the plantations, and they would tear you to pieces, gentle as they are. It is easy for you to come here and advise us to ruin our industry; if we were so foolish as to take your advice we should have to bear the punishment of our folly, while you, when you saw the misery and desolation you had caused, would be able to hoist sail and leave us."

Captain Adam saw that the old man was too angry to listen to him any more, so he went away, first having obtained leave to come back in two or three days with a scheme which he said would prevent all the disasters which the chief had predicted as sure to follow the abandonment of the palm plantations.

Captain Adam set to work to get this plan into shape: the main feature of it was not to abandon the plantations suddenly, but gradually to transfer the labour they now absorbed to more profitable occupations. In two years he calculated that the whole 400 people now employed in the palm plantations might be growing spices and coffee enough to form a valuable export trade, and that at no time during the process of transition should any of the labourers be out of employment. They were to be removed from the palm plantations in companies of fifty at once; an eighth of the entire population was at the same time to be permitted the privilege of having windows; and in return for this favour the non-oil growers were to provide the ex-oil growers with necessary food and clothing till the first crops of coffee and spices could be sold, when the ex-oil growers would be quite independent of the help of their neighbours. Captain Adam was very pleased with his scheme; it was as clear as daylight, he thought, that it would make everybody in the island better off, and that owing to the great fertility of the land the transition from the palm to the coffee plantations could be carried out with very little difficulty.

A time was appointed for him to explain his plan to the council of the chiefs. They listened to him patiently till he came to the part where he tried to make it clear that in two years the palm plantations might be entirely abandoned; and then they rose in great wrath, and shouted him down. A comparative calm followed in a few minutes, when the old chief, to whom he had first broached the subject, rose and said: "Your scheme would ruin us; the palm plantations are our own property; you propose to us that they should be abandoned, and that we should submit to ruin and degradation. Leave our calm and peaceful island for ever: it was an evil day that ever you set foot in it."

Captain Adam blamed himself very much for not having found out that the palm plantations were the private property of the council, for he knew men too well to think they would ever pass laws involving loss to themselves. He tried to say something about compensation, and about other crops being raised on the land where the palm trees now stood; but they would listen to nothing, and ordered him forthwith to leave the island. This order he was obliged to obey, but not before he had attempted to interest the general population in his scheme. His success with the people, however, was not greater than with the chiefs; he tried to put the advantages of sunlight, good tools, ploughs, and scythes, and cheap clothing in as striking a light as possible; he did his best to show the people that they would have all these good things in exchange for their unwholesome oil. But they only saw in his plan the destruction of the most important industry in the island, and they joined heartily with their chiefs in driving him to his ship.

He left the Srimats full of indignation at their folly, and as far as he knows they are still living in a pestilential atmosphere, the darkness of which is feebly illumined by their ill-smelling oil-lamps.

This story is an illustration of the fact that when you have once got protection it is impossible to get rid of it without injuring the people who have invested their capital and labour in the protected industry. The case of the Srimats was an extreme one. The foreign competition with which the palm-oil industry was threatened would have swept the palm-owners out of the market in one day. The sun not only offered a vastly superior article, but he was ready to make a free gift of it to all comers. What tradesman could compete against such odds? The existence of protection interests a number of people in its maintenance, although its maintenance often fatally impoverishes the entire community. What protection really does is to take away labour and capital from those employments where they would produce the greatest return, in order to confine them to industries where they are comparatively unremunerative. The Srimats would have done the best thing possible with their capital and labour if they had cultivated the spices, for which their land was particularly well suited. They threw away the advantages which nature had freely bestowed upon them, and by one of the most extraordinary cases of protection in the world imprisoned their capital and labour in an industry where it was absolutely unproductive of wealth to themselves or anyone else. And this in a modified degree is what happens in every case where a native industry is protected against foreign competition. Home-grown beet-root sugar, in France, is protected against the competition of West Indian cane sugar by a heavy import duty. If the duty were removed, West Indian sugar would undersell the French sugar. The effect of the duty is that all people who live in France pay more dearly for their sugar than they otherwise would; and that a certain amount of French capital and labour is driven into an industry in which it can only be made profitable by taxing those who consume the commodity produced by it. Nature gives more help to the production of sugar in the West

Indies than in France. Just as the sun was ready to supply the Srimats gratuitously with light, so the sun, the soil, and the climate, in the West Indies, perform gratuitously a great part of the work of producing sugar. This free gift the French might profit by if they would. But they say, "No; we won't be under such an obligation to nature, we will not take from her more help than she can give us in our own country." And so they refuse the greater and accept the smaller gift; just as the Srimats refused to take their light as a free gift from the sun, although they could not have grown their palm trees without his aid.

II.

The Shipwrecked Sailors.

Division of labour—Exchange—Are luxurious expenditure and waste good for trade?—Demand for commodities not a demand for labour—Demand and supply—Competition—Value and price—Elements of value—Free trade—The influence of increase of population on the cost of food—The principle of diminishing productiveness of extractive industries—Increasing cost of agricultural products may be accompanied by a diminishing cost of manufacturing products.

ONCE Captain Adam and some twenty of the passengers and crew of a sailing vessel were shipwrecked on a small uninhabited island in the Pacific. They were like Robinson Crusoe in one respect, which was, that they were fortunate enough to be able to save a number of things off the wreck, which they found to be of immense value and comfort. They were not able, like Robinson Crusoe, to go to their vessel before it broke up, and ransack it for the most useful things they could find; they got nothing that was not washed ashore, so they obtained altogether a very motley collection. Their rule was that whoever found anything was the owner of it, or, as it was more tersely expressed by the sailors, "Findings is keepings." The consequence of this rule was that there was very soon a great deal of buying and selling in the little community. Three men, for instance, succeeded in hauling to the shore a case which proved to contain twelve dozen pairs of boots of various sizes. This bit of good luck made them for a time quite the capitalists of the little community. In exchange for the boots, which were very sorely needed by their companions, they obtained a share of the most useful things that had been found. One man, who had found a case of spirits, came and offered a bottle of rum for a pair of boots. Another man had found a box of carpenter's tools, and it so happened that he was quite unable to use them to advantage, whereas one of the men who had found the boots was a carpenter by trade, and very much longed to possess the box of tools. A harder bargain never was struck than between these two men. The carpenter began by offering a pair of boots in exchange for the tools. "Nay," said the other, "boots are very well in their way; but they tell me you have got scores of 'em; and I reckon I can get something more than a pair of boots for my tools. Besides, I rather think I shall keep the tools myself. I am not such a fool but what I can drive a nail and use a saw almost as well as if I had done nothing else all my life." They were not able to come to any agreement, and the finder of the tools so far got the best of it, that he succeeded in getting a pair of boots from one of the other men in exchange for the loan of the saw for one day. By this time the little colony were busy in making themselves small wooden huts in which they slept, and where they found shelter from storms. As the process of building these huts went on, Green, the man who had found the tools, discovered that by lending them he could obtain either a share in what had been found by the others, or an equivalent in the form of labour. "Lend us the axe and mallet, old fellow," said one, "and I'll give you three dinners off the fish I catch in the morning;" or perhaps it was, "Lend me the saw and plane to-day, and you shall have half the number of planks that I am able to make in the time."

It was not long before Green, and indeed all the party, found that amateur carpentering is a very expensive process. One man chopped his toe off with the axe when he was trying to cut down a tree, and was laid up for a month. The planks, that had been sawn and planed by an apothecary's apprentice, might have deserved to be sent to a museum of curiosities; but they were certainly not in their right place when he tried to make them into a door and keep out the blasts of a tropical hurricane. But the shipwrecked sailors not only found that it was easier to cut and bruise their own toes and fingers than to convert the young palms into decent habitations; there was another, and perhaps a more serious disadvantage attaching to their unskilful work. Green often found when the tools were returned to him that they had suffered almost as severely as those who had attempted to use them. The teeth of the saw were bent, the edge of the axe was turned, the chisel was broken in half, and almost as many nails were broken and bent, or were knocked in in the wrong places, as were driven home exactly on the spot where they were wanted. These various misfortunes made everybody see how much better things would go on if the carpenter did all the carpentering that was needed by the little colony. If the carpenter hired the tools of Green, Green would lose nothing, for the carpenter could give him more for the loan of them than anyone else, because no one could make such good use of them as the carpenter. The carpenter would also be a gainer, because he would then be able to turn his skill in his trade to the best account, and would get all his wants supplied by his companions in return for the services he rendered to them. Finally, the entire colony would gain by the carpenter having the use of the tools; for instead of chopping off their toes, bruising their fingers, and spoiling the tools, with the worst possible result in the carpentering line, they now saved their own skin, the tools were not injured, their carpentering was well done; and in return for the services of the carpenter, every man and woman gave him a share of what he or she was most skilful in producing or most fortunate in finding. The advantage everyone enjoyed from this division of labour was apparent: the carpenter had no need to leave his trade in order to go hunting or fishing; he had very little skill in these pursuits, and had sometimes been out all day without bringing home enough for supper. Here was folly and waste of time! If he had stayed at home he could have finished Jack Collins's hut, and made a strong bench for Mrs. Collins; while Jack, who knows the ways of every bird that flies and every fish that swims, would bring back enough game and fish to last all the next day for himself, his wife, the carpenter, and half-a-dozen others; and Mrs. Collins, the swiftest of knitters, whose bench would have been a strange production if she had made it herself, would have made a pair of strong socks for the carpenter in return for the bench. It was therefore agreed on all hands that everyone should find out what he or she could do best, and stick to it. Jack Collins and two others were able to provide the whole company with as much fish and game as they could eat. Mrs. Collins was in great request in consequence of her skill in knitting, mending, and patching. One man, who had been a blacksmith, found that the best thing he could do was to melt down all pieces of old iron, copper, and other metals that were washed up with the wreck, and convert them into nails, saucepans, &c. He was also able to repair the damage done by the unskilful use of the carpenter's tools. Everyone, in fact, found that there was some way in which he or she could be more useful than in others. There were two children, who were always hard at work collecting firewood for the blacksmith and for cooking; and they also searched about on the shore for pieces of the wreck that had copper bolts in them, or any fragments of metal, which the smith was not long in converting into pots and pans.

There was one man who had been a passenger on the ill-fated ship, who was certainly not very well adapted to a Robinson Crusoe life. Mr. Davies, on a desert island, was about as much at home as "a whale in a field of clover." He was a man who had always acted on the principle, that to have a new hat once a week, new lavender kid-gloves every day, innumerable suits of clothes, no one of which he ever wore more than three times, to smoke the most expensive cigars, to drink the rarest wines, to eat the most costly meats, and consume fruits and vegetables only when they were entirely out of season, was good for trade. He now found, however, that this way of encouraging trade was not appreciated by his companions; he expected that the best of everything on the island would be brought to him for his acceptance, and that if he approved it he would have the opportunity of buying it and paying for it with a cheque drawn on a New York banker. His disgust, when his cheques were refused, and when the dainties he coveted became the possession of those who could give either labour or other commodities in return, was amusing to witness. One day hunger overcame his laziness, and he consented to superintend the broiling of a quantity of fish, on condition that he was to share in the eating of the supper. The weather had been stormy, and fishing had been difficult and very unproductive for some time past; when therefore a large haul was made there was a great deal of rejoicing, and everyone promised himself a good supper. Great therefore was the wrath when it was found that Mr. Davies had left the fish on the fire to broil while he went to sleep under a tree, and that consequently it was burnt to a cinder. Everybody was cross, and no one was less so when Mr. Davies excused himself by saying that burning fish was good for trade. He was quite prepared to argue the point, and turning to Collins and the other men who had caught the fish, he said, "You have nothing to complain of; you have sold the fish that is burnt, and have got all kinds of things in exchange for it; and now everybody wants some more, and you will be able to sell twice as much and get twice as many things in return as you would if the first lot had not been spoiled." "According to you then, Davies," said the captain, "the best thing for all of us would be to pitch half of what we are able to scrape together into the fire. Collins would not have found any difficulty in disposing of all the fish he caught to-day. The only effect of your carelessness is, that everybody will have to pay twice over for their supper to-night, and consequently they will be less able to pay for their dinners to-morrow than they would otherwise have been. For instance, the carpenter has been at work all day making clothes'-pegs for Mrs. Collins; he has made two dozen; for one dozen he had bought his share of the fish you have spoiled; now he will have to give the other dozen with which he would have been able to buy his dinner to-morrow. So burning the fish has reduced his power of buying what he wants by the value of what he gave for his supper; and what is true of him is true of everybody who had bought a share in the food you spoiled. He is no better off now than he would have been if he had only made a dozen instead of two dozen clothes'-pegs; so I think the less you say about wasting things being good for trade, the better."

Poor Mr. Davies was a long time before he could get over his notion that the way to make everybody well off was for him to do nothing, and to eat as much as he could, and to destroy the products of his companions' labour as fast as possible. He was only prevented acting on this opinion by the stubborn resistance that was shown to it on the part of his comrades; and he had to learn by degrees that a demand for commodities is not a demand for labour; and that the only demand for labour is that which is ready to supply commodities to the labourer in exchange for those which his toil produces. If you demand commodities, you must supply the labourer who produces them with an equivalent value of some other commodities or services. So demand and supply cannot increase independently of each other. If demand increases, supply must increase at the same time. For instance, if Mrs. Collins wants the carpenter to make her a bedstead, she must supply him with a whole suit of clothes; if her demand increases, and she wants, besides the bedstead, two chairs, she must supply him not only with a suit of clothes, but with a dozen pairs of knitted socks into the bargain. It will be noticed, that if production increases, demand also increases; if, for example, Mrs. Collins finds out a new way of knitting by means of which she can make three pairs of socks in the same time that she previously employed to make two pairs, her power of buying the products of other people's labour is increased 50 per cent. Her demand for these products therefore increases in consequence of the increased productiveness of her own labour. It accordingly happens that general prosperity and an increased demand for commodities nearly always go together; but the increased demand is not the cause of the increased prosperity. On the contrary, the increase of production gives those who benefit by it greater power to purchase the products of other kinds of labour; in other words, increased prosperity makes a greater demand for commodities possible.

As the shipwrecked sailors on the island gradually got cleverer in the work they had undertaken to do, their labour became more productive; and directly their labour was more productive a greater number of things were bought and sold, or exchanged. In other words, when a greater amount of wealth was produced, there was a corresponding increase in the demand for, and the supply of, commodities.

Two or three of the sailors were fortunate enough to find a bag of wheat only slightly damaged by the salt water. As may be imagined, it was most carefully dried in the sun, and every grain was valued much more than if it had been made of solid gold. A favourable piece of ground was looked out; it was then dug by the men who had found the wheat, and when what they all thought the best season for sowing had arrived, the precious grains were carefully deposited in the rich soil. When the first green blades appeared above the ground there was a general feeling of rejoicing. It was many months since anyone on the island had tasted bread; for some time after the shipwreck a plentiful supply of sailors' biscuits had been washed ashore; but these were now all finished, or if any more were found on the beach they were so sodden with salt water that they were quite uneatable. Everyone, therefore, looked forward very eagerly to the time when the wheat would be converted into loaves of bread. The fortunate possessors of the small wheat-field spent nearly all their time in looking after it. In the dry season while the wheat was young, they watered it; and when it was nearly ripe, fearing it would be damaged by the violence of a tropical storm, they erected a strong bamboo fence all round it to protect it from the wind. At last the precious grains were ripe, and, after setting apart a due quantity for seed, it was bartered away at an enormously high value for the possessions and labour of the other inhabitants of the little colony. Everyone very much enjoyed his first bit of bread; but there was no doubt that its flavour was improved by the circumstances under which it was eaten. To tell the truth, it was sour and coarse, and the general remark about it soon was, not "How very nice the bread is," but "There's no doubt it will be much better next season." Nearly everyone had an opinion of his own why the first crop was not a success; one said it was watered too much when it was young; another said the bamboo fence kept the sun off it when it was ripening; another said the earth was not properly prepared. The result of all these differences of opinion was, that about a dozen people laid by part of the wheat they had procured for their own eating, resolving to use it as seed, and grow a crop of their own upon their own principles. The result was a great improvement, both in the quantity and quality of the wheat. Those who planted wheat the second season learnt by the experience of those who had planted it in the first season; and not only was there a yield four times as great, but the grain itself was much better in size and quality. As the seasons succeeded each other the growing of wheat became one of the staple industries of the island; and of course the more was produced the more easy it was to obtain it; that is to say, those who did not grow it for themselves could obtain it in exchange for a much smaller quantity of labour or commodities of their own manufacture than was possible after the first harvest had been gathered in. If the people on the island had carried on their exchanges by the means of money, we should say that the price of wheat went down very rapidly when a greater quantity was grown and when improved methods of cultivation were adopted. As, however, they did not use money, but exchanged commodities for commodities, we cannot speak of *price* declining; for price means the value of anything measured in money. But we can say that the value of the wheat went down; for value is measured by the rate at which commodities exchange for each other. Exchange without the use of money is called barter; and every schoolboy is familiar with its practice, which he calls "chopping." When we say, therefore, that the value of the wheat declined, it is not meant that the wheat became less useful; value, in political economy, is not determined by usefulness, although if a thing were utterly useless it would have no value whatever; the value of a thing is what you can get in exchange for it; everything therefore that has value must not only be useful in itself, but there must also be some degree of difficulty in obtaining it. The greater this difficulty is, the higher is the value of the commodity. Thus, the difficulty of getting a sea-water bath in your house when you are staying at the sea-side is very small; it consists only of carrying the water a short distance from the sea. The value of the water would therefore be very small. But if you want a sea-water bath in Central Africa, the difficulty in obtaining it would be very great, and the value of the water proportionately increased. The usefulness of the bath in the two places may be imagined to be exactly the same; the difference in value is caused by difference in the difficulty of obtaining it. The value of the wheat therefore gradually declined, because the difficulty of obtaining it became less. This decline in value was a very good thing for the islanders, because it showed that they were able to provide themselves with a staple of food at a smaller cost of labour and self-denial.

When the trade of wheat-growing was firmly established on the island a very important discovery was made by some of the sailors, who had contrived to manufacture a boat for fishing purposes. In the course of one of their fishing expeditions they landed on an adjacent island, and as they had to wait there some time before leaving, for the turn of the tide, they began to look about them to see if they could find anything worth taking home. They were struck by the appearance of some trees which grew in this island in great numbers, but which they had never seen in their own island. These trees were from fifteen to twenty feet high, with immense leaves of a beautiful shining green. Some of the leaves were ten feet long and three feet broad; in the midst of these leaves rose large stems bearing clusters of fruit.

Not knowing what these trees were, the sailors were afraid to eat the fruit, but they pulled some down, and wrapping it round with its leaves, they returned to their own island. When they showed it to the captain, he recognized it directly as the fruit of one of the most valuable kinds of plantain trees. Every part of this tree serves some useful purpose in providing food and clothing for man. The fruit can be eaten either ripe or unripe: if it is gathered before it is ripe, it can be peeled, sliced, dried in the sun, and ground to a powder; prepared in this way an excellent flour is obtained, which serves all the purposes of wheat-flour. The ripe fruit is very good raw; and it may also be eaten boiled or roasted, or fried with butter. A very wholesome drink is also made by soaking the fruit in water, something after the manner in which malt is converted into beer. Wine can also be made by fermenting the juice of the fruit. The top of the stalk boiled is a good vegetable; and the fibre of the leaves can be made into strong cloth. It has been calculated that the food-producing power of the plantain is 133 times greater than that of wheat. Its cultivation requires very little labour; it is generally propagated by suckers, which attain their full growth in about ten months after they are planted; and they go on bearing for fifteen or twenty years.

The ease with which these trees could be cultivated, and the number of purposes they were capable of serving, made their discovery the most important event that had taken place since the shipwreck. Calling the whole of the company together, the captain explained to them that they had now a new source of obtaining both food and clothing; that no more labour need be expended in the cultivation of corn; they would be able to provide themselves with a variety of excellent food free of all labour except that of bringing the fruit from the place where it grew to their own island; and he added that they might confidently expect soon to have plantain-trees round their own settlement. A hearty cheer rose from some of the sailors when the captain finished; but he noticed that the cheer was not universal, and looking round he saw that those who did not join in the general rejoicing were men who had given the principal part of their time and labour to the cultivation of corn. Some of these men had ripe crops now standing on the ground, which they had expected presently to be able to exchange for the clothing, fish, game, and other articles procured by the labour of their companions; and it occurred to the captain, when he saw their downcast faces, that there would no longer be any demand for corn when bread could be obtained so much more easily from a plant, the cultivation of which had cost no man either toil or self-denial; and that consequently the discovery of the plantain-trees, though adding so much to the general wealth and prosperity, would be attended by some real suffering on the part of the men who had grown wheat. Just as the captain was thinking of this, one of the principal corn-growers got up and said :—" I consider, sir, that we are going on too fast when we say that finding these trees is such a wonderfully good thing for us all. I and my mates have been slaving away these three years to make corn grow here, and at last we have made it grow. Now, for the protection of native industry, I say you oughtn't to flood our market with food that costs next to nothing, while the food we are able to produce has cost us many a hard day's work, besides involving an immense amount of risk and anxiety. It is impossible our home-grown corn can compete against these foreign plantains; we can't produce food in our own market with four times the labour that it will take to bring the plantains over in the boats. The corn-trade, the principal industry we have, will be completely ruined, and all those engaged in it will lose their ordinary means of supplying their wants. I say, sir, that it would be a much better thing for us to make firewood of every plantain we can find than to destroy the corn-trade, on which so much of our prosperity has hitherto depended."

When he had finished speaking there was a murmur of disapprobation from the majority; but the corn-growers, and those dependent on them, greeted what he said with clapping of hands and other signs of approval. Every eye was now turned on the captain for a reply. He said, "I am not going to deny, and I think no one will deny, that those among us who have ripe corn now in the market will not get in exchange for it what they would have got if these plantain-trees had not been found, and that the labour it has been necessary to give to the cultivation of corn will be needed no longer. But that is not everything that we ought to think of. We do not live to labour, but we labour in order to live—that is, we labour to supply our wants. If our wants can be supplied with a smaller amount of labour than we have hitherto been compelled to give, it is so much the better for us all. We can either labour less and enjoy the same degree of comfort; or we can labour as much as we did before and obtain a larger number of comforts and gratifications. Those who have up to this time given so many weeks and months of labour to the cultivation of corn complain that their labour is now superseded. But this means, that what formerly it took many months of labour to procure can now be obtained as the result of a few hours' exertion. The corn-growers, so far as they are corn-consumers, will profit as much as all the rest of us in obtaining food as an almost free gift, as it were, from nature; every mouthful of bread which they eat in future will represent only a hundredth part of the sacrifice of labour and abstinence which was required to produce the wheaten bread. They will also share to the full the advantage which the discovery of the plantain-tree gives us in obtaining a new beverage, a much needed means of replenishing our clothing, and in preparing a great variety of vegetable food. It is true they will not obtain as much as they expected for their standing crops. But they will obtain something, and the increased wealth with which these plantain-trees have suddenly endowed us will enable us to give more in exchange for what we want than we could otherwise have done. There is no fear that our home-grown wheat will be wasted. As the demand for bread has been satisfied in a cheaper market, let me recommend those who are the possessors of wheat to try if they cannot turn their property to good account, both for themselves and us, by introducing a luxury that we should all very much appreciate; I mean beer. Almost all grain can be turned into malt. Malting is a very simple process; and if when the malt is made, the brewing is successfully carried out, I am sure the value of the beer to its owners will more than compensate them for any inconvenience that they may suffer from being suddenly deprived of their usual means of selling their wheat. If the brewing is a success, the wheat-growers will be able to exchange the beer for the best of everything that we all produce. What would we not give for a good glass of ale after a hard day's work? If it fails, of course there will be a loss to be endured; then the growing of wheat will have to be given up, and those who have till now been our wheat-growers will be able to give their labour to some other industry. Depend upon it, it will not be difficult to find new kinds of paying work; making the fibre of the plantain into cloth will require a vast amount of patient industry, and any labour that can be saved in other employments will be most profitably occupied in weaving, and first of all in manufacturing the necessary apparatus for weaving."

When the captain had finished, the corn-growers still looked very glum. Their loss on their standing crops they thought was certain, and their profits to be made out of brewing and weaving were at present only castles in the air. They soon found, however, that their grumbling was no good; there was no chance of inducing their companions to endure unnecessary privations in order, artificially, to create a market for their wheat;—if they had the power, no doubt they would have passed a law, like the English corn laws, and similar in principle to all measures for the protection of native industry, to prevent the introduction into their island of all food that could be procured at a less cost than the food grown at home. They would have liked to put an import duty on the plantains, so as to raise their price above the price of the home-grown corn; then native industry would be protected and foreign competition effectually excluded. Fortunately, however, they had no power to prevent their neighbours from supplying their wants at the lowest possible cost: *i.e.*, at the least possible sacrifice of labour and self-denial. They were, therefore, compelled to endure what they could not cure. It was impossible for them to deny that the new flour made very good bread, or that the other dishes that were made from the plantain-fruit formed a very pleasant variety in their fare. Some of them began to prepare their wheat for the brewing process which the captain had recommended; but they did this with the air of those who considered themselves very hardly treated. Some of them said they didn't believe it was possible to make malt of anything but barley, and they therefore exchanged their wheat for anything they could get for it. Meanwhile, they began to work at preparing the plantain-fibre for weaving, and before long they succeeded in producing a coarse, but very strong and useful cloth, which they disposed of to their neighbours in exchange for the products of other industry. In less than a year there was not one of the former corn-growers who did not confess, if not to his neighbours, at least to himself, that he had been a great gainer by the discovery of the plantain-trees. The degree of comfort, and even luxury, possessed by everyone on the island had increased fourfold in consequence of finding these friendly trees. Food was now secured to every one almost free of cost; the greater part of the labour that it was formerly necessary to give to obtain daily bread was now set free, and it found new employment in those industries that added to the comfort and enjoyment of life. The growing of wheat was not given up; the brewing was very successful, and, as may be imagined, the beer exchanged at a very high rate of value for other commodities. The wheat-fields, therefore, became as profitable as ever. The brewers were a little jealous at first of the favour with which the plantain-beer and plantain-wine were received; but they gradually learnt that they did not profit by the poverty, but by the prosperity of their neighbours: every discovery or invention that made the community richer made each one among them easier in his circumstances: each one had more time to devote to other kinds of industry; there was, consequently, a greater supply of commodities, and those who possessed this increased supply were anxious to dispose of what they did not require for their own consumption; that is to say, the increased supply led to an increased demand. Hence, the brewers and all the other producers of commodities found that the better off their neighbours were, the brisker was the general demand for commodities, and the greater was the number of exchanges effected.

Some years passed away, and the little colony made rapid progress, not only in riches and industrial skill, but also in numbers. There were several families of young children who had been born since the shipwreck, and who were fast growing up to be men and women. Ten years after the shipwreck it was found, that although they had lost two of their comrades by death, the islanders had increased in numbers from twenty-three to fifty. It is obvious, therefore, that at the end of the ten years, about twice as much food was needed to satisfy daily wants as was required immediately after the shipwreck. It is true that they found food much easier to obtain than they had at first. If there were more mouths to feed, there were also more hands to work; and they had besides had time to find out the best and most profitable way of working. Nevertheless, one result of the increased number of mouths to feed was that food had to be obtained at a proportionately increased sacrifice of time and labour. At first, for instance, the skilful fisherman only went to those pools where the fish were most abundant; and from these, in favourable weather, he could catch enough in a few hours to feed everyone on the island; but now these pools were not such good fishing-ground as they used to be; the stock of fish there had become to a great extent exhausted; and it was necessary, when fish were needed, either to fish for a greater number of hours in these favourite old pools, or to make long and perhaps dangerous journeys to distant fisheries, where the labour of the fisherman was more abundantly rewarded than it now was in the old and easily accessible pools. The fish that were brought home as the result of these distant fishing excursions exchanged for other commodities in proportion to the labour endured and danger incurred by those who procured them. For instance, the carpenter at the end of the ten years had to give a greater value of the articles he produced, in exchange for a meal of fish, than he had when first he began to live by his carpentering. The danger and difficulty of fishing had increased; there was no danger in the carpenter's work, and its difficulty had been reduced by the adoption of various means of saving labour, and by improvements in the tools. Therefore, at the end of the ten years, the products of the carpenter's and the fisherman's labour exchanged in a different proportion to that at which they had exchanged at first. The carpenter's work had become less costly; the fish had become more costly; so that an amount of fish which the carpenter could once obtain in exchange for half-a-dozen washer-womens' clothes-pegs, or a couple of broomhandles, he could not now purchase, except by offering what had cost him twice as much labour—such as a child's stool, or a pair of oars. The same difference in relative value occurred in other industries. Speaking generally, all the food-producing industries became more and more costly; that is to say, to obtain a given amount of food, it became necessary to give a greater amount of labour and sacrifice, and in some cases to incur a greater amount of danger; whereas in the manufacturing industries cost either remained stationary or was actually reduced. In a given number of hours of labour, the carpenter, for instance, produced as much now as he did ten years ago; in a given number of hours of labour, those who wove the plantain-fibre into cloth, produced half as much again as they did when they first applied themselves to the work. This resulted from the improved appliances which they now brought to their industry, and also to the greater skill with which the fibre was prepared for weaving. Fishing was not the only trade that had become less productive in proportion to the amount of labour expended upon it; in a less degree, the same increase of cost had affected the value of the staple product of the island, the plantain. At first, when the plantains were discovered, the islanders only used the fruit of those trees that were in the most convenient situations. They did not row ten miles for their plantain grove, when they could find an equally productive one by rowing five. They did not trouble to gather the smaller fruits, when they could fill their baskets so much more quickly by gathering only the larger specimens. By and by, however, they found that the nearest plantations were beginning to be less productive; then some of the men whose business it was to gather plantains went further away in search of new plantations, and those who remained filled their baskets with the smaller fruit, which at first had not been worth the trouble of gathering. After this, fears were felt by the islanders that they were using up their stock of food too rapidly, and that precautions should be taken to prevent a scarcity in future years. Then a large piece of ground in the most favourable situation was cleared, and plantain suckers were put in, to form a new plantation. Afterwards the same process was repeated on a piece of ground less favourably situated; and so it happened that the amount of labour necessary to procure a certain quantity of plantains steadily and necessarily increased. And as the labour of procuring food increased, whilst the labour of producing manufactured commodities either remained stationary or was reduced, the exchange value of food compared with manufactured articles steadily increased. It is no doubt true that the cost of obtaining food would have tended to increase, if the numbers of the colony had remained the same. They would still have gathered their plantains at first in those places where they could be found with least trouble, and as these best places began to be used up they would find that the same amount of food could only be obtained through a greater amount of labour than was at first necessary. In fishing, they would have gone first to the nearest and fullest pools; and it is probable that by degrees they would find that they must either fish for a greater number of hours, or move to more distant fisheries, if they wished to obtain as much as they did at first. It is evident, however, that this diminishing productiveness of food-producing industries (and of all "extractive" industries, under which term are included agriculture, mining, and fishing) is made much more rapid than it otherwise would be by an increasing population. Another thing was observed by those whose business it was to bring to the island a sufficient supply of plantains. Doubling the amount of labour engaged in gathering the plantains did not even at first double the quantity of fruit they were able to bring home. At first, five men were able in two hours to gather as many plantains as would fill their boat. But they could not in four hours gather enough to fill two boats. Because, in the first two hours, they would gather the largest, and those that were most easily reached. In the second two hours, they had to gather smaller specimens, and those that grew in places where they were not so quickly reached. If you took four boys to a cherry-tree, and told them they might have as many cherries as they could gather in twenty minutes, they would get in that time many more than four other boys who were allowed to attack the tree afterwards for the same time and on the same conditions. The first party of boys would gather all the cherries that could be most easily and quickly reached; the second party would have to climb to the topmost branches and strip off every tiny fruit. So it was with our islanders and their plantains: every succeeding year an additional quantity of food was required, and it had to be procured at a constantly increasing cost of labour. It may perhaps be thought that as the labour necessary to supply a given quantity of the plantain fruit steadily increased, and thereby increased the cost of obtaining food, therefore the cost of obtaining clothing must also have increased, as the cloth used on the island was made of the plantain fibre. It is true that the cost of the fibre did increase, for the same reason that the cost of the fruit increased; but the cost of the cloth, that is, the number of hours of labour necessary from first to last to produce a piece of cloth, was

E

actually reduced. Only a very small part of the labour necessary to make the cloth consisted in bringing the fibre from the place where it grew to the place where it was manufactured; nineteen-twentieths of the labour required to produce cloth was engaged in preparing the raw fibre, and in weaving it after this preparatory process was complete. A few years' experience in these manufacturing industries caused such an improvement in the implements used, and in the skill with which they were handled, that although the labour of procuring the raw fibre had increased, the total labour of producing a piece of cloth had very much diminished, and its exchange value was therefore proportionately reduced.

There is nothing more about the little colony that I can remember, except that after being on the island for twenty years, they were visited by H.M.S. *Leo*, the captain of which offered to take away half the colony in his vessel, and to send for the other half in a few months. Only twelve of them, however, wished to leave at all. The others thanked the captain, but said they didn't wish to leave their island and begin life over again on the other side of the world. The visit of the ship, however, was a splendid thing for the colony, for the captain gave them a number of things which they could not otherwise have procured. Amongst these were two guns, powder, and shot, a quantity of old iron, a case of books, writing-paper, pens and ink; and last, but most important of all, two pigs, two goats, two sheep, and some fowls. Captain Adam was one of the twelve who went away in the *Leo*. He brought letters to England to the relations of those who were left on the island. When I saw him he was thinking of going back to it himself to end his life there; he says he has never felt quite at home since he left it; he thinks that if he took out with him machinery and tools, and a few skilled artisans, the island might soon become one of the richest and most flourishing settlements in the world.

III.

Isle Pleasant.

Money is a universal measure of value, and medium of exchange—The convenience of using money instead of making exchanges by barter—The substance used as money should possess four qualities: it should be valuable in itself, its value should as far as possible be steady, it should possess great value in small bulk, and it should be capable of being sub-divided without reducing its value—Credit—The effect of credit on prices—The elasticity which various forms of credit give to the currency tends to check fluctuations in prices caused by active or slack trade—The influence of money in promoting division of labour—Shops.

SOME years after the last chapter was written I had some letters from Captain Adam, dated from Isle Pleasant, the name that had been given to the settlement. He had carried out his plan of returning to the island, taking with him a steam-engine, some spinning-jennies, and looms for weaving, besides a large collection of books, cutlery, and other articles. He was accompanied by two engineers, and by six Lancashire factory women. Captain Adam was very confident that the latter would be able to produce a cloth from the plantain fibre very superior to any that had been made with the rough machinery and unskilled labour of the first inhabitants of Isle Pleasant; and he also was very certain that the engineers would be very valuable additions to the community. On arriving at the island he found that great progress had been made in a variety of ways during his absence. The most striking change that had been made was the introduction of the use of money. As the way in which it had been introduced was rather curious, it shall be described.

The Pleasant people, as they liked to call themselves, had long been grumbling at the inconvenience of carrying out a great number of exchanges by means of barter; the man who had a basket of plantains to dispose of, and who wished to obtain in exchange a knitted jersey, would find perhaps that Mrs. Collins, the woman who was the best hand at making these jerseys, had more plantains already in stock than she expected to want for the next four months, and that although she would be quite willing to give a jersey in exchange for an ironing-board and a washtub, she would not give anything at all for an unnecessary addition to her stock of plantains. Now, if they used money, this inconvenience would be completely avoided; the man who had the plantains would sell them for money to whoever happened to want them; he would go with the money in his hand to Mrs. Collins, and buy the jersey that he wished for; and she could then go with this same money to the carpenter, and buy her ironing-board and washtub. There was a great deal of talk about the inconvenience of having no money to make purchases with, and two or three suggestions were made to adopt some natural product of the island as money, and make all exchanges by of means this product. The plan was even tried of using cocoa-nuts for money; they were not at all plentiful in the island; to procure them required a considerable amount of exertion, as they grew in distant places, and they were very generally valued for their own sakes, as the milk they contained was very refreshing, and the nut itself was wholesome and nutritious. They had, therefore, the two necessary elements of value, *i.e.* they were useful in themselves, and there was some difficulty in obtaining them; and every substance used as money must have these qualities, for it is obvious that people will not exchange away products which have cost them labour and self-denial to obtain in return a substance which can be obtained without effort, or which serves no useful purpose. But, although the cocoa-nuts possessed one quality, "intrinsic value," which made it possible to use them as money for the purpose of carrying on all exchanges, in two other qualities which should characterize the substance used as money they were found wanting, to a degree that soon led to the abandonment of the idea that they could be used as money. In the first place, although they had considerable intrinsic value, this value varied very much from time to time. Their value in use was pretty constant, but the difficulty of obtaining them varied exceedingly: at one time, nearly all the cocoa-nuts fit for use would be consumed; those remaining on the trees would be unripe, then the value of the few that were fit for use would rise immensely. At another time, a hurricane would blow down a dozen of the trees, and their fruit could then be picked up with much less labour than when it was necessary to climb to the top of the trees to get them. This would cause the value of the nuts rapidly to decline for a time, when, perhaps, some other accident would again make their value as rapidly rise. These variations in value led to very unpleasant consequences; for instance, Collins, perhaps, would want to buy a bedstead of the carpenter, and agree to give him a certain number of cocoa-nuts for it when it was finished. It took a month to finish, and during that time cocoa-nuts, instead of being plentiful and easy to obtain, had become very scarce, owing to the trees having been attacked by monkeys, who had carried off two-thirds of the nuts. Collins, therefore, found at the end of the month that it was very difficult for him to carry out his part of the bargain, and that he could only obtain the cocoa-nuts with which he had to make his payment by twice the amount of labour and trouble that they had cost a month before; he therefore had in reality to give twice as much for his bedstead as he had agreed to do when the bargain was struck. But besides the inconvenience arising from their frequent variations in value, the cocoa-nuts were extremely unsuited to be used as money in another respect. Suppose that a cocoa-nut represents the value of a shilling, and Mrs. Collins is going out to make purchases of her different neighbours. She wants several yards of plantain cloth, some books for her children, some reels of plantain thread, a strong wooden-box, a set of tea-cups and some mugs (I forgot to say that the Pleasant people had set up a very good pottery), and some pots and pans from the smith. Altogether her purchases come to the value of 5*l*. To pay this sum she would have to take with her 100 cocoa-nuts. Fancy a lady going out to pay her bills with a bag of 100 cocoa-nuts on her back! The bulk of cocoa-nuts in proportion to their value was so great that it formed the strongest possible objection to their use as the universal medium of exchange; but their unsuitability was made evident in another way

If Mrs. Collins sent her little girl to buy one reel of thread, price 1d., she would have to give $\frac{1}{12}$th part of a cocoa-nut in exchange for it. Now every part of a cocoa-nut has some value, and as the value of every part, except the shell, gets less from the time the shell is opened, it was very difficult to use the nuts to make small payments. If a cocoa-nut were divided into twelve equally valuable parts, every one of these, except the shell, would be less valuable a day after it was opened than when first it was divided, because the pieces exposed to the air would become first dry and chippy, and then positively bad. All these inconveniences were so great, that the Pleasanters determined they would go on with their old plan of making their exchanges by barter, until they could find some substance which would be more suitable to use as money than the cocoa-nuts. About this time fortune was once more their friend. One day a young lad, who was a splendid swimmer, was diving on a side of the island where the coast was steep and rocky, when he discovered a large chest, which had apparently been long under water, firmly fixed between two rocks. He tried to move it, but without success; he then told his discovery to several other boys, who were as good swimmers as himself, and they went together with a strong rope, which they managed to pass round the chest, and while those above pulled at the rope, those who were in the water did their best to get it out of the nook where it was so firmly wedged in; but all their efforts were unsuccessful, and they were obliged to return home without their prize. On reaching the settlement, they told their friends what they had been doing, and on the next day a party of about five-and-twenty men and boys started off, armed with ropes, crowbars, and axes; for they were determined that, if they could not bring the chest ashore, they would break it up, and bring its contents, whatever they were, to dry land. They agreed that the contents should, if worth anything, be shared among the members of the party: the boy who first found the chest was to have a double share, and those who had been with him on the second day's expedition were to have a share and a half. After a great deal of hard work, in which those on shore gave a long pull, a strong pull, and a pull altogether, many times without result, whilst the divers shoved and pushed below, the chest suddenly lunged over, and as it moved the bottom fell out, and a bright stream of gold and silver money spread itself out on the rocks. Up went the divers to tell the news, each one carrying a handful of coin as a specimen of the spoil. Great was the joy of the whole party on hearing what had been found. Two of the number, who were chosen by general consent, because they were thoroughly good fellows who would be sure to see fair-play done to everyone, were made the guardians of the store; they took charge of it till every gold piece had been brought to land; and then they counted it, and divided it into the shares that had been previously agreed to. The coins were English, and there were some of nearly every description; altogether the amount brought to land came to 7,450*l*. There were twenty-five of the party, one of whom was to have two shares, and eight of whom were to have a share and a half; the whole sum was, therefore, divided into thirty equal lots of 248*l.* 6*s.* 8*d.* each. The boy who first discovered the chest took two of these shares, or 496*l.* 13*s.* 4*d.* The eight boys who worked with him on the second day, each took a share and a half, or 372*l.* 10*s.*, and the sixteen who remained took one share each, of 248*l.* 6*s.* 8*d.*

When they returned to their companions, the rejoicing at the discovery that had been made was universal. The want of money for carrying on exchanges had long been felt, and the coin was therefore much more valued than it would have been if it had been found when the trade of the islanders with each other was so limited that it could be conducted by barter without inconvenience. It may perhaps be thought that the discovery of the gold and silver was of no benefit to the islanders in general, but only to those among them who were so fortunate as to be its actual finders. It soon, however, became evident that those who had found the money profited by their discovery exactly in proportion as they parted with it. It was of no service at all to them if they shut it up in a box or hid it in the earth; it was useful only when they parted with it to their companions for the meat, clothing, and other articles produced by them. By this natural process, brought about by the desire of those who had money to buy with it the result of the labour of others, and the desire of those who had no money to procure it by offering commodities or services for it, a general distribution of the gold and silver which had been found was in a few months made among the whole of the inhabitants of Isle Pleasant. At first, before this distribution was effected, and while the money was in the hands of a few, the price obtained for articles was exceedingly high. Some of the finders of the money were so foolish as to leave off working, and as they were obliged to obtain food and clothing by some means or other, large prices for these necessaries were extracted from them. A man who had done nothing to obtain a dinner for himself would give a sovereign to share in the meal prepared by his neighbour, rather than remain hungry when he had a bag full of gold. Gradually, however, as the money became more evenly distributed, the relative prices of things settled down into correspondence with their real value. Thus in the old days of barter, a pair of oars, which represented one day's work of the carpenter, would exchange for twice as much plantain bread as a wooden bowl which only cost the carpenter half a day's work; the value of the pair of oars was, therefore, twice that of the wooden bowl. And now that money was in general use, the price of the oars was double that of the bowl. What the scale of prices actually should be was controlled by three things: 1st, by the amount of money in circulation; 2dly, by the quantity of things that were bought and sold for money; and 3dly, by the number of times commodities were bought and sold before they were used. It is evident that the amount of money in circulation must have an influence on general prices. Suppose that the same number of people are receiving wages, that the same quantity of commodities are bought and sold the same number of times, and that the money used for paying wages and buying commodities is suddenly doubled, is it not evident that under these circumstances prices and wages would go up, or, in other words, that the purchasing power of money would go down? When the islanders tried to use cocoa-nuts for money, this fact was perfectly well understood. Anything that made cocoa-nuts more plentiful, lowered their value and their purchasing power; the average of general prices was controlled by the supply of the circulating medium. In the island the supply of money could not be increased; no more discoveries of chests of gold and silver were made. But the trade and commerce of the island steadily increased, more commodities were produced, and bought and sold; and as the trade of the community became more complex, these commodities were bought and sold a greater number of times before they were consumed. These circumstances caused a corresponding increase in the value of money, or, in other words, a corresponding decline in general prices. The number of uses for money was extended; the number of times each individual had occasion to employ money became greater; therefore the demand for money increased, but the supply remained fixed and stationary; it was thus inevitable that its exchange value should be increased. The trade of Isle Pleasant therefore presented the spectacle of steady growth, of a continual increase in wealth and prosperity, together with a correspondingly steady decline in general prices. This is no exceptional phenomenon. The same tendency for an increasing trade to produce a decline in prices exists in all countries, but it is counteracted by the circumstance that the supply of money and of the substitutes for money is capable of being increased in a degree corresponding, or even more than corresponding, with the increased use for money caused by commercial development. Thus in England the immense growth of trade since the repeal of the corn laws and the development of the railway system (1846—50), has been accompanied by a rise in general prices varying, according to different authorities, from 15 to 25 per cent. But this would not have been pos-

F

sible if it had not been that, owing to the great gold discoveries in Australia and California (in 1848—52), the annual yield of gold was suddenly increased from about 8,000,000*l.* to 27,000,000*l.*; and in one year (1856) it even rose to more than 32,000,000*l.* If the development of trade had taken place without any increase in the supply of gold, prices must very materially have declined; on the other hand, if trade had been stationary during this sudden multiplication of the annual production of gold, there must have been a very rapid rise in general prices. In Isle Pleasant, as we have seen, the supply of money was absolutely limited, and therefore each increase in the number of trading transactions caused the value of money to rise and prices to fall. Six months after the money was discovered, the islanders transacted a certain amount of buying and selling, a certain number of people were receiving wages, and for these purposes they used their 7,450*l.* Ten years afterwards twice as many people were receiving wages, three times as many commodities were produced and bought and sold.

The amount of money used to carry on this great increase of trade was exactly the same, 7,450*l*. Hence it is evident that the amount of money used in each transaction must have declined, or, in other words, prices and wages must have gone down. At the same time population increased; so there were not merely a larger number of trading transactions to be performed with the same amount of money; there were also a larger number of people among whom this fixed amount of money was distributed. Not only therefore did less money change hands every time any particular purchase was made, but the aggregate of money possessed by each individual was, on the average, reduced; at the same time it must be remembered that this decline in prices, wages, and in property in money, was not merely accompanied by, but was caused by the growth of Isle Pleasant in real riches and prosperity.

It was pointed out that when the islanders attempted to make use of cocoa-nuts as money, great inconvenience was caused by their frequent and sudden variations in value. A man who had promised to pay a debt in a hundred cocoa-nuts in six months' time would perhaps find that, owing to the destruction of the nuts by monkeys, or to the discovery of an additional number of the trees, the difficulty of obtaining cocoa-nuts had become during the six months either much greater or much less than it was when he made his bargain; and in this way commercial transactions that extended over any lengthened period of time were liable to great uncertainty owing to the fluctuations in value of the substance used as money.

Inconvenience, similar in character, though not so great in degree, was now felt to attend the steady rise in the value of gold and silver in Isle Pleasant. If a man made an agreement to pay a certain sum of money, say 10*l.* a-year, for ten years as the rent of a house that had been built by one of his neighbours, it was quite certain that, owing to the gradual rise in value of gold, his rent would in reality increase each year; till at the end of the ten years the same amount of money would perhaps represent twice as much value in goods and labour as it did when the bargain was struck. In this way all bargains that extended over a period of months or years had something of a very speculative or even gambling character. People felt pretty sure prices and wages would go on declining, but they could not be certain how rapid the decline would be, nor how far it would go. A temporary check to production caused by some unforeseen misfortune might for a time prevent prices falling at all; or, on the other hand, some industrial discovery might give a fresh and unforeseen impetus to production, and the decline might be much greater and more rapid than could have been anticipated. It might be said that no real harm is done by the introduction of this uncertainty into the terms of all bargains; for whatever is lost by one party to the bargain is gained by the other. If John Smith promises to pay 20*l.* to Robert Williams at the end of twelve months, and if this 20*l.* is worth 10 per cent. more at the end of the year than either of them expected it would be when the bargain was made, John Smith is 10 per cent. poorer than he expected to be by his bargain; but Robert Williams is 10 per cent. richer, and therefore it may be said that on the whole no harm is done. It must however be remembered that when a bargain is made, both parties to it expect to gain by the transaction; if they did not they would have no motive for entering into the agreement. They not only both expect to gain, but if this expectation on either of their parts is disappointed, a blow is struck at the trade and prosperity of the community. The 10 per cent. lost by John Smith will probably take away all his profit or even convert it into a loss: it will be no consolation to him to know that Robert Williams has made 10 per cent. more profit than he expected. The burnt child dreads the fire; and after suffering this unexpected loss John Smith will be very timid in entering into bargains in future; and his loss will also produce a similar timidity in others; and as bargaining is a game which two must play at, a blow will thus be struck at the development of trade.

The disadvantage of the continual and rapid rise in value of gold and silver in Isle Pleasant, at length induced the inhabitants to use various substitutes for money which had an effect similar to that which would have been produced if additions had been made to the amount of coin in circulation: these substitutes for money tended to check the fall in prices and wages, and thus to make the value of money more uniform. The plan generally adopted was that of giving (when a purchase was made) a written promise to pay in money at the end of a certain time, instead of making the payment in cash at once. It may seem curious that these written promises to pay in gold and silver at the end of a short time could have had any effect as substitutes for money; since it may be thought that the payment in money was only temporarily deferred; but as a matter of fact these written promises to pay often had the effect of preventing the use of money in effecting exchanges altogether, and commodities in this way were exchanged for commodities without the transfer either of gold or silver, just as in the old days of barter. For example, Collins would buy of Cox, a plantain cloth weaver, 5*l.* worth of cloth, and would give him a written promise to pay him five sovereigns at the end of four weeks; before the four weeks are over Mrs. Collins has made a complete suit of clothes for Cox and each of his four children; for which service Cox gives her a written promise to pay her five sovereigns in a fortnight's time. Now if Mr. and Mrs. Collins cancel Cox's debt to them, Cox agrees to cancel Collins's debt to him; so the cloth and the suits of clothes exchange for one another without the transfer of any money on either side, just as they would have done in the time when all exchanges were made by barter. It sometimes happened, of course, that two people were indebted to each other, but not for exactly the same amount. Thus Cox may have promised to pay the carpenter 1*l.*, while the carpenter may have promised to pay Cox 18*s.* In this case, the balance, 2*s.*, will have to be paid in money by Cox to the carpenter; but nevertheless it must be remembered that an amount of buying has taken place amounting in all to 1*l.* 18*s.*, and that it has been accomplished by the transfer of only 2*s.* in money, the rest of the exchange having been effected by barter. Sometimes it happened that of three or four people each was indebted, and each had a debt owing to him of equal value but not from the same person. Their position will perhaps be made clear by the accompanying figure. The arrows → show to whom each of the four is indebted :—

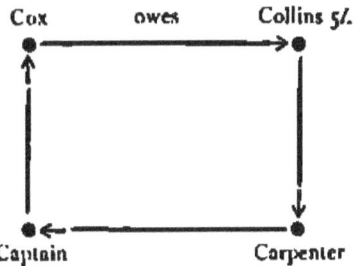

Each of these four men owes and is owed 5*l.* Cox owes Collins 5*l.*, and is owed the same sum by the captain, and so on all round. Now these four men, by exchanging the written promises to pay which they have respectively made, can cancel all their debts without the exchange of one farthing of coin. *Money's worth* has already been exchanged between them, and each owes and is owed an exactly similar amount ; if then they agree to cancel each other's debts the exchange is effected virtually by barter, and the only service which money gives to the transaction is that which it affords as a "measure of value." As a medium of exchange it is not used at all.

The method just described of dispensing with the use of money by means of written promises to pay which are exchanged for and cancel each other, grew with the growing wealth and prosperity of Isle Pleasant ; and thus an effectual check was put upon the tendency of prices to fall as a consequence of the increased number of exchanges which were caused by the progress of industry and manufactures. The more active trade was, the greater was the number of bills of exchange (or promises to pay) that were used to make purchases. Thus a virtual addition was made to the currency at the very time when it was most needed ; and these additions to the currency ceased to exist as soon as trade became slack; that is, as soon as the need that had called them forth ceased to operate.

In England an immense amount of trade is carried on without the exchange of coin, by means of the various forms of credit, which are all, in one way or another, promises to pay. In the London clearing-house, the place where the cheques drawn on different banks are daily exchanged for each other, as much as 2,000,000,000*l*. worth of cheques are exchanged in the course of a single year, without the transfer of one penny of money: that is to say, that buying or selling to the amount of 2,000,000,000*l*. takes place in one year in England by means of cheques alone, without the transfer of any gold or silver coin whatever. This substitute for money has the same effect upon prices as if a large addition were made to the money in circulation. In the same way bills of exchange (which are promises to pay, at a certain date, made by one merchant to another), and bank-notes (which are promises to pay on demand made by the banker to the possessor of the note), form virtual additions to the currency ; and if they were withdrawn or ceased to be used, one of two things would happen : either prices would decline, or an addition of gold and silver would have to be made to the currency, equal in exchange power to the forms of credit withdrawn from circulation.

The changes introduced into Isle Pleasant through the use of money and credit in carrying on exchanges were very important. Division of labour prevailed much more completely than before. The risk, in the days of barter, of not being able to get immediately the things that you wanted in exchange for the things you were willing to dispose of, was so great that people did not like to be entirely dependent for their supplies of food, for instance, on the labour of others. Hence, nearly everyone, no matter what his or her regular occupation was, devoted some time to the cultivation of food stuffs. But when the use of money became general this was no longer necessary; everybody sold the product of his or her industry for money, and could then use this money to buy the products of the labour of others. A man who had a pair of oars to dispose of and who wanted a coat, had no longer to search here and there for a man who had a coat to give and who wished to take the oars in exchange. He sold his oars to anyone who would buy them for money, and with this money he purchased the coat from anyone who had one to dispose of. As division of labour thus became more and more complete, shops were opened, so that everyone who wanted food, clothing, fishing-tackle, or any other commodity that was made by the inhabitants of the island, knew exactly where to go to buy it. In this way there was a great saving of time and trouble, and thus another addition was made to the industrial well-being of Isle Pleasant. For among the services which labour renders to production, must not be forgotten that of bringing commodities to the places where they are wanted, and to places where people who want them know where to find them. It is a great waste if a man, whose labour can in one day produce commodities worth 10s., is compelled to spend an hour every day in seeking about for people who will sell him what he wants for his daily food. The collection of different kinds of commodities in shops is a very real and considerable service to industry.

It may be imagined, then, how great a change Captain Adam found when he returned to Isle Pleasant. He left the islanders trading with each other under all the difficulties of the system of barter; he came back and found them buying and selling with money, using various forms of credit which acted as substitutes for money, and carrying on retail businesses in well-arranged shops. The changes that took place in their industrial system after Captain Adam's return will be described in the next chapter.

IV.

The Islanders' Experience of Foreign Trade.

The benefit of foreign trade does not consist in causing an increasing quantity of gold and silver to be sent to the exporting country, but in enabling each country to supply its wants at a reduced cost by giving it the opportunity of applying a larger portion of its labour and capital to those industries in which it has the greatest advantage over other nations, or at any rate to those industries in which its disadvantage is the smallest—Foreign trade an extension of the principle of division of labour.

CAPTAIN ADAM'S return in a ship of his own manned by a crew of English sailors, and laden with machinery and mechanics, was hailed with great joy by everyone in the island. The ship was a special attraction to every boy in Isle Pleasant, and the sailors soon became general favourites. There were a dozen lads who anxiously looked forward to the first outward-bound journey of the *Carrier Pigeon*, as the ship was called, for each had a hope that

he would be wanted to make one of the crew.
It was not many weeks after Captain Adam's
return that the *Carrier Pigeon* set sail for San
Francisco laden with some of the produce of
nearly every industry on the island. These
were plantains and plantain flour, cloth, plantain wine, many articles of clothing, some very
fine specimens of cabinet work sent from the
carpenter's shop, and many other things, too
numerous to be set down here. Before sailing, the man who had been appointed captain
of the *Carrier Pigeon* went to see each one of
the men and women who had contributed something to the cargo, to know what they wished
to have brought back in exchange for the
things they had sent. He went first to the
carpenter, who had reckoned that the things
he had sent would fetch 20*l.* in San Francisco.
"Your things are worth fully 20*l.*," said the
sailor; "what shall I bring you back?" "Why,
bring me 20*l.*," said the carpenter, "or as much
more as you can get. I will give you a shilling
out of every pound you bring me home." "All
right," replied the sailor, and the bargain was

struck. Everyone made a similar arrangement; for it was thought that when the ship returned and all those who had sent goods received a sum of money, they would be able to buy of their neighbours anything they wished for, and that this would be much better than spending the price of the goods in San Francisco. "We can make things for ourselves," they said; "so what's the good of buying them of the Yankees?"

So the *Carrier Pigeon* set sail, laden with agricultural produce and manufactured articles, that, speaking roughly, had cost every man, woman, and child on Isle Pleasant a month's labour. Everyone had sent something, and everyone anxiously waited for the return of the ship that would bring with it so much extra wealth and enjoyment (it was thought) to the whole island. If children asked their parents for a treat, the answer was, "Wait till the ship comes home." The Collinses wanted to add another room to their house, but they said they would wait till the ship came home, as they would then have money to buy the best materials and hire the most skilled labour. At last the *Carrier Pigeon* came in sight; and a few hours more brought it into the little natural harbour on the south side of the island. The captain was soon on shore. There was no cargo to unload, and therefore there was no delay. A sheet of paper, on which was written down the sum realized by the sale of the goods and the amount due to each person, and a heavy cash-box, were all that it was necessary to bring ashore. To the great joy of the islanders, their goods had sold for nearly double what they had expected. "Gold pieces are as thick as blackberries in San Francisco," said the captain. When the list was read out and the cash-box opened, everyone received a good round sum of money. The carpenter had 40*l.*, Mr. and Mrs. Collins 37*l.*, the best weaver 20*l.* Everybody had something, and even the little children received half-crowns and shillings for toys they had made and sent away to San Francisco to be sold.

After the first rejoicings at the return of the ship were over, everyone began to think what use he could make of his newly-gained wealth. One old man, who had waited till the ship came home before he supplied himself with a new jersey that he very much needed, came up to Mrs. Collins with money in his hand to buy one. "I'm very sorry, I'm sure," she said, "that I can't supply you. I sent away half-a-dozen, that would have fitted you exactly, in the *Carrier Pigeon*, and since that I've been busy making new suits for my husband and children, and so I haven't got any jerseys for sale at present." "Perhaps you'll be having some in a week or so," said the old man. "Well, I can't say, I'm sure," said she; "they say the *Carrier Pigeon* is to sail again in three weeks, and I want to make up a good parcel of things to send in it, for we get such good prices over there." "Well," he said, "if it's the price you're thinking of, I will give you as much for a jersey as it would sell for in San Francisco." "That's 30s.," she said. Now that was just double what the old man had paid for his last jersey; but he had a great deal more money now than he had then, and he wanted the jersey very badly, so rather than go without it he promised Mrs. Collins the 30*s.*, and she agreed to let him have the jersey in a week. He went away feeling that he had been very unfortunate, and that he wasn't so much better off as he expected to be in consequence of his pocketful of silver.

The Collinses, now they had received the 37*l.*, and were also receiving higher prices in the island itself for everything they could make, began to think they should do well to buy the materials they wanted for the addition to their house. Collins went to the carpenter to hear if he could come and work for them, and to see if he could buy planks, doors, and other woodwork. He found the carpenter hard at work on a beautiful carved side-board, on which he was working, as he said, "almost night and day." "Who is it for?" said Collins. "Why, for the *Carrier Pigeon*, to be sure," replied the carpenter; "she's the best customer I've got." When Collins explained what he wanted, the carpenter shook his head. "Impossible," he said; "I can't do it; it's as much as ever I shall do to finish this by the time the *Carrier Pigeon* sails, and I expect it will fetch a hundred guineas in San Francisco. I've been at work on it ever since the ship left for the first time, five weeks to-day; I shall be lucky if I finish it in another three; but it'll bring me a hundred guineas if it brings me a penny." "A hundred guineas," gasped Collins, "for eight weeks' work! Why, leaving out the Sundays, that's more than a guinea a day." "Right you are," said the carpenter, chuckling; "and that's what I shall want to earn now, whatever I work at and whoever I work for." Poor Collins went away, and said to his wife, "We must do without that new room—the carpenter won't work now under a guinea a day; he says he can make that by sending things to San Francisco, and that he won't work for less." Mrs. Collins was very angry. She had been out to buy cloth and various things that she wanted for the making of the clothes she intended to send away in the ship. She had found everything either about twice the price that it had been before the return of the ship, or that it was not to be had at any price. Not only were the goods that were sent away much dearer, but the things that were intended only for home consumption had gone up in price also. Many of the people who had been cultivators of a kind of plantain that was eaten raw, and which was a very favourite food in the island, had given up selling the fresh fruit; they were now busy in making it into a rich preserve which they intended to send away in the *Carrier Pigeon;* so of course those that were sold raw were much dearer: first, because their owners would have sent them all away if they did not receive a higher price at home than formerly prevailed; secondly, because those who wished to buy them had now more money in their possession in consequence of the gold brought back in the ship, and therefore they had it in their power to give the increased price demanded.

Although everyone worked away with great energy to provide a second cargo for the *Carrier Pigeon*, the delight that had been caused by the return of the ship had now quite died away. Nobody understood how it was, but everyone knew that, although he had more money than before, he was not so well off. The money had lost a great part of its purchasing power; it was more difficult than formerly to obtain supplies of the necessaries and comforts of life. It is not difficult for us to see how this happened; they had sent away the things that really support life and add to its enjoyments; they had parted with the food and clothing that a month's labour from the whole population had been able to produce. And what had they received in return? That which would feed no hungry mouths, and cover no bare backs. The gold that was brought to them would have tended to produce a rise in prices even if it had been a free gift and if no commodities had been sent away in exchange for it. But now that the available supply of commodities for home consumption was reduced whilst the supply of money was increased, of course money became relatively less valuable; and when money and commodities were exchanged—or in other words, when purchases were made—more money had to be given for the same commodities than heretofore.

The fact that in sending their manufactures and "the kindly fruits of the earth" to a foreign country and receiving in return certain pieces of metal stamped in a particular way, they were parting with the things that constitute real wealth and prosperity without receiving any adequate return, at length became painfully evident to all the inhabitants of Isle Pleasant. The more food and clothing that was sent to San Francisco, the less remained to be enjoyed by the islanders; at the same time the steady flow of gold and silver into the island, together with a falling off in the domestic trade, caused a very great rise both in prices and wages.

At last the captain of the *Carrier Pigeon* solved the difficulty that had arisen out of the manner in which the foreign trade of Isle Pleasant was carried on. It had always been a matter of great regret to him that the *Carrier Pigeon* should make her return journey without a cargo. It was wasting all that a voyage cost to bring her home empty. Now he observed that at first when he began his voyages, nearly everything sold for much more money in San Francisco than in Isle Pleasant; yet even at first there were some things, such as boots, that were much cheaper in San Francisco than in Isle Pleasant. Then as prices and wages rapidly advanced on the island, the prices of the exports she sent to San Francisco declined there; so it soon happened that there was not more difference in the cost, for instance, of plantain flour in San Francisco and Isle Pleasant than was sufficient to provide a remuneration for the labour and risk of bringing it from one place to the other. When this point was reached of approximate equality in prices between the two places, the trade, as long as it consisted entirely of exports from Isle Pleasant paid for in money by San Francisco, began to fall off. For if they could get as much money by selling their goods at home, the islanders had no inducement to send them abroad. Now, however, the captain resolved that the *Carrier Pigeon* should make her return journey empty no longer. The next time he was in San Francisco he laid out all the money he had earned as commissions on his former voyages in commodities which either could not be produced at all in the island, or could only be produced by much more labour there than at San Francisco. Among the former articles were wines, brandy, various useful medicines, books, and cutlery; among the latter were boots and all leather goods, wool, tallow, hides, and cloth. Getting a large cargo of these things on board the *Carrier Pigeon*, he set sail for the island. When he arrived he was pleased to find that his cargo of goods commanded a ready sale; the islanders were very pleased with the San Franciscan things. "Look at these boots," said one; "I bought them for 18*s*. I couldn't have got them here under 30*s*., and they'd not have been near such good ones." Mrs. Collins was delighted with the cloth; she could buy for 3*s*. a yard cloth much superior to that which was made in the island and sold there for 4*s*. 6*d*. The result of the general satisfaction was that the captain was commissioned not to bring back

money after his next voyage to the owners of
the goods exported to California, but to spend
the price of the goods in things that could
be produced at a greater advantage there than
on the island. As this system of trade became
general, little or no money passed between the
island and San Francisco; the exports being
made to pay for the imports without the transfer
of coin from one country to another. It will
be seen that both San Francisco and Isle
Pleasant were benefited by trade carried on in
this manner, for the island now shared in those
commodities which San Francisco had a special
advantage in producing, whilst San Francisco
enjoyed a similar benefit in sharing those articles
for the production of which the island was specially well adapted. Thus in the old days before
any foreign trade was established, it took an
islander the labour of eight days to produce
a very rough and clumsy pair of boots; now
by getting them in San Francisco, he could
obtain them by sending there as much plantain
flour as cost him four days' labour. Measured
in the labour necessary to obtain them, the

boots, therefore, only cost him half as much as before. In the same way the San Franciscans could obtain plantain preserves, cocoa-nuts, and palm oil from the island at the sacrifice of half the labour, compared with that which the things would have cost to produce in their own country.

In this way it was proved to the islanders that foreign trade, to be permanent and beneficial, must be in the nature of an exchange of commodities for commodities. If one country sends commodities and is paid entirely in money, it parts with its real wealth without receiving any substantial advantage; and if this kind of trade is carried on for any length of time, prices go up in the exporting country, and go down in the importing country, till at last prices in each country are made equal, and in this case the motive for trade carried on in this way ceases to exist. For when the islanders could obtain no more money for their goods in San Francisco than at home, they naturally preferred to sell them at home rather than to run the risk and to bear the delay of sending their commodities to a distant country. When foreign trade is not reciprocal (that is, when one country only sends commodities and is paid by the other in money) the advantage is all on one side, and therefore it has no permanence or stability; for the country which reaps no real advantage naturally gets tired of a trade from which it derives no benefit, and after a while such a trade is certain to cease. But when two countries exchange with each other the commodities which each has some comparative facility for producing, each country is permanently benefited, and therefore such a trade will be lasting and stable in its character. It is a first condition of any kind of permanent trade that each party to it shall be really benefited by the transaction; otherwise the one who is not benefited will withdraw from the trade, which would consequently come to an end. We have seen, then, that foreign trade, although the amount of it may be measured in money, must in reality be an exchange of commodities for commodities. But we have scarcely yet inquired "what commodities?" It will perhaps be thought that each country will always send away those commodities for the production of which she has greater facilities than the other country to which the commodities are sent. For instance, Isle Pleasant has a great advantage over San Francisco in the production of plantains. Plantains can be grown on the island with one-fourth the labour that it would be necessary to employ to grow them in San Francisco; whereas boots can be produced at one-half the labour in San Francisco that it would be necessary to give to produce them in Isle Pleasant. Therefore a profitable trade to both countries can be established if San Francisco sends boots to Isle Pleasant, and receives plantains in return. This is very true, but it does not always happen that one country has an absolute advantage over the other in any one particular branch of industry. Sometimes, owing to the greater fertility of the soil and other natural advantages, such as geographical position and the skill and industry of the population, one country has greater facility than the other with which it trades in producing every kind of commodity;

that is to say, that the same amount of labour
and capital produces a greater return in every
branch of industry in one country than in
another. Yet between two such countries a
trade advantageous to each may be carried on.
We will suppose that Isle Pleasant loses its
special advantage in producing plantains, and
when this advantage is lost, that San Francisco
can produce all commodities at a smaller sacrifice of labour and capital than it takes to produce them in the island. It may be thought
that in this case the San Franciscans would no
longer wish to supply any of their wants from
the products of the island, since they have
themselves an advantage over the islanders in
every branch of industry. This, however, will
not be the case. Although the San Franciscans
have the advantage in every kind of industry,
their advantage is less in some industries than
in others; and if their advantage over the
islanders is less, for instance, in the production
of matting than in the production of leather
goods, a trade might be set up which would
be permanently advantageous to each country

in which San Franciscan leather was exchanged for the matting produced on the island. Let it be supposed that in San Francisco leather can be made for one-fifth of the sacrifice of labour and capital that is necessary to its production on the island; but that matting can be made on the island at only a slightly greater sacrifice of labour and capital (say one-tenth more) than at San Francisco. Then, if there is no trade between the two countries, it follows that these commodities exchange for each other at different rates of value in the two countries. Leather being so very difficult to produce in the island, exchanges there at a very high value compared with matting: a pair of boots, we will say, would exchange in the island for forty yards of matting. But at San Francisco, although both matting and leather can be produced with less capital and labour than on the island, the San Franciscans have a much greater advantage over the islanders in the production of leather than in the production of matting; the comparative value of the two commodities is therefore very different at San

Francisco, for there a pair of boots can be obtained in exchange for five yards of matting. Now if this is 'the case, it is obvious that a trade in these two articles might be set up between the two countries, and would be very advantageous to both. We will suppose that the islanders send their matting to San Francisco, and that in the first instance they obtain for it the full value of matting, measured in boots, that prevails in that country. This, as we have seen, is at the rate of five yards of matting for one pair of boots, or eight times as high a value as the matting obtains in the island. But if the trade is conducted in this way, San' Francisco does not obtain any advantage from it; she does not get her matting any cheaper than she did before, and she will have no inducement unless she gains something on the transaction beyond what she previously obtained to send away her leather goods to a foreign country. The islanders, therefore, will find that if they are to obtain a market in San Francisco for all the matting they are willing

H

to send there, they must consent to a reduction in its exchange value. Instead of getting eight pairs of boots for their forty yards of matting, they will perhaps eventually have to consent to take only four; and at this rate of exchange we may imagine that a permanent trade is set up between the two countries. If this is the case, the island abandons altogether the production of an article (boots) in which her industrial disadvantages are the greatest, and devotes a larger portion of her labour and capital to the production of the commodity (matting) in which her industrial disadvantages are the least. In the same way, San Francisco gives up a trade in which her superiority is small to devote herself to one in which it is great; and by this means the industrial efficiency of each country is brought to its highest possible perfection. The advantage to each country is very apparent; the islanders now obtain boots at one-fourth of the labour and trouble which it was formerly necessary to give for them. The San Franciscans, before the trade with the island was established, gave a pair of boots for five yards of matting; a pair of boots, after the trade is set up, exchanges for ten yards of matting, so they now obtain their matting in exchange for one-half of the labour and trouble that they had formerly to give for it.

The whole secret of the advantage of foreign trade is, that it enables each country to apply its labour and capital as far as possible to those industries in which its advantages are the greatest, or in which its disadvantages are the least. Considered in this way, free trade between nations is an extension of the principle of division of labour. It sets nations free to do those things which they can do best; just as division of labour sets individual men and women free to do that kind of work which they can do best. England can obtain wine, tea, silk, and many other foreign products, at a much less sacrifice on her own part, by producing iron and manufactured cotton goods, than she would have to give if she attempted to produce these foreign goods on her own soil; just as everyone who earns his own living can best obtain the necessaries and comforts of life by applying himself to the one particular occupation in which he can do his best: he exchanges the result of his labour for the result of the labour of other people, and by this means a person of quite ordinary capacity obtains a degree of comfort and luxury which no man, however clever and however industrious he might be, could furnish himself with if he relied solely on what he was able to produce directly with his own labour.

In the example just given of the exchange of boots and matting between Isle Pleasant and San Francisco, it was shown that both places gained by the establishment of the trade. The islanders got their boots at one-fourth, and the San Franciscans their matting at one-half of the previous cost. But it must not be supposed that this benefit was obtained quite free of all counterbalancing disadvantages. The graziers and tanners on the island had a great deal to say against the use of San Franciscan leather; the matting manufacturers at San Francisco felt themselves very hardly treated when they were driven out of the market by the matting-makers from Isle Pleasant. Both these sets of people suffered a real loss in their businesses by the establishment of the trade between the two countries. They had gradually to transfer their labour and capital to other occupations, and this could not be done without considerable loss. It must, however, be remembered, that this loss could by no possibility be avoided except by inflicting a much more than corresponding loss on all the purchasers of boots on the island, and on all the purchasers of matting at San Francisco. If the San Franciscan boots had been excluded from the island, the graziers and tanners would have been saved a certain amount of loss, anxiety, and annoyance; but, on the other hand, every man, woman, and child would have had to give four times as much for shoe-leather as was necessary; or, in other words, a heavy poll-tax would have been imposed in order to please a small section of the inhabitants, and to enable them to confine a certain portion of the capital and labour of the island to an industry in which they were less productive of wealth than they would be if they were applied to the manufacture of matting. In the same way, the matting manufacturers of San Francisco could only have been saved the loss consequent on the introduction of the matting from Isle Pleasant by a similar process of distributing a much heavier loss over all the consumers of matting at San Francisco. It should also be remembered, that the loss inflicted on special classes of manufacturers by foreign competition is for the most part only temporary. It drives capital and labour to the industries in which they are most productive, and eventually by this means the very men who at first were most injured by foreign competition are frequently among the chief gainers by it. Whereas the loss inflicted by shutting out foreign competition is permanent; it locks up capital and labour in industries where they are comparatively unproductive, and thus detracts from the industrial efficiency of the nation. One sometimes hears the expression, when a person is doing work for which he is obviously unfitted, "It is like putting a race-horse to plough." The exclusion of foreign competition, or the "protection of native industry," as it is called, generally means a process very like setting a race-horse to plough. The poor creature cannot plough as well as a bullock; but the bullock is a foreigner, so we will have none of his ploughing, and we will put a heavy tax on all land ploughed by bullocks, in order that the race-horse may always continue to do the work for which he is so ill suited.

The islanders had come face to face with the question of "protection to native industry" when the plantain groves were discovered. The free-traders, then, had carried the day; and now that the question was raised again by the graziers and tanners in respect of the San Franciscan leather, the free-traders were equally successful; the islanders resolutely determined to maintain the trade, and when the choice was presented to them between a temporary loss on a few among their number, and a permanent loss on the whole of the inhabitants of the island, they had little difficulty in selecting the former as the less of two evils.

THE END.

BEDFORD STREET, COVENT GARDEN, LONDON.
September 1874.

MACMILLAN & CO.'S CATALOGUE of Works in BELLES LETTRES, including Poetry, Fiction, etc.

Allingham.—LAURENCE BLOOMFIELD IN IRELAND; or, the New Landlord. By WILLIAM ALLINGHAM. New and Cheaper Issue, with a Preface. Fcap. 8vo. cloth. 4*s.* 6*d.*
  "*It is vital with the national character. . . . . It has something of Pope's point and Goldsmith's simplicity, touched to a more modern issue.*"—ATHENÆUM.

An Ancient City, and other Poems.—By A NATIVE OF SURREY. Extra fcap. 8vo. 6*s.*

Archer.—CHRISTINA NORTH. By E. M. ARCHER. Two vols. Crown 8vo. 21*s.*
  "*The work of a clever, cultivated person, wielding a practised pen. The characters are drawn with force and precision, the dialogue is easy: the whole book displays powers of pathos and humour, and a shrewd knowledge of men and things.*"—SPECTATOR.

Arnold.—THE COMPLETE POETICAL WORKS. Vol. I. NARRATIVE AND ELEGIAC POEMS. Vol. II. DRAMATIC AND LYRIC POEMS. By MATTHEW ARNOLD. Extra fcap. 8vo. Price 6*s.* each.
  The two volumes comprehend the First and Second Series of the Poems, and the New Poems. "*Thyrsis is a poem of perfect delight, exquisite in grave tenderness of reminiscence, rich in breadth of western light, breathing full the spirit of gray and ancient Oxford.*"—SATURDAY REVIEW.

Atkinson.—AN ART TOUR TO THE NORTHERN CAPITALS OF EUROPE. By J. BEAVINGTON ATKINSON. 8vo. 12*s.*
  "*We can highly recommend it; not only for the valuable information it gives on the special subjects to which it is dedicated, but also for the interesting episodes of travel which are interwoven with, and lighten, the weightier matters of judicious and varied criticism on art and artists in northern capitals.*"—ART JOURNAL.

Baker.—CAST UP BY THE SEA; OR, THE ADVENTURES OF NED GREY. By SIR SAMUEL BAKER, M.A., F.R.G.S. With Illustrations by HUARD. Fifth Edition. Crown 8vo. cloth gilt. 7*s.* 6*d.*
  "*An admirable tale of adventure, of marvellous incidents, wild exploits, and terrible dénouements.*"—DAILY NEWS. "*A story of adventure by sea and land in the good old style.*"—PALL MALL GAZETTE.

Baring-Gould.—Works by S. BARING-GOULD, M.A. :—
  IN EXITU ISRAEL. An Historical Novel. Two Vols. 8vo. 2*s.*
  "*Full of the most exciting incidents and ably portrayed char*

BELLES LETTRES.

Baring-Gould—*continued.*
abounding in beautifully attractive legends, and relieved by descriptions fresh, vivid, and truth-like."—WESTMINSTER REVIEW.
LEGENDS OF OLD TESTAMENT CHARACTERS, from the Talmud and other sources. Two vols. Crown 8vo. 16s.
Vol. I. Adam to Abraham. Vol. II. Melchizedek to Zachariah.
"*These volumes contain much that is very strange, and, to the ordinary English reader, very novel.*"—DAILY NEWS.

Barker.—Works by LADY BARKER:—
"*Lady Barker is an unrivalled story-teller.*"—GUARDIAN.
STATION LIFE IN NEW ZEALAND. New and Cheaper Edition. Crown 8vo. 3s. 6d.
"*We have never read a more truthful or a pleasanter little book.*"—ATHENÆUM.
SPRING COMEDIES. STORIES.
CONTENTS:—A Wedding Story—A Stupid Story—A Scotch Story—A Man's Story. Crown 8vo. 7s. 6d.
"*Lady Barker is endowed with a rare and delicate gift for narrating stories,—she has the faculty of throwing even into her printed narrative a soft and pleasant tone, which goes far to make the reader think the subject or the matter immaterial, so long as the author will go on telling stories for his benefit.*"—ATHENÆUM.
STORIES ABOUT:— With Six Illustrations. Third Edition. Extra fcap. 8vo. 4s. 6d.
This volume contains several entertaining stories about Monkeys, Jamaica, Camp Life, Dogs, Boys, &c. "There is not a tale in the book which can fail to please children as well as their elders."—PALL MALL GAZETTE.
A CHRISTMAS CAKE IN FOUR QUARTERS. With Illustrations by JELLICOE. Second Edition. Ex. fcap. 8vo. cloth gilt. 4s. 6d.
"*Contains just the stories that children should be told. 'Christmas Cake' is a delightful Christmas book.*"—GLOBE.
RIBBON STORIES. With Illustrations by C. O. MURRAY. Second Edition. Extra fcap. 8vo. cloth gilt. 4s. 6d.
"*We cannot too highly commend. It is exceedingly happy and original in the plan, and the graceful fancies of its pages, merry and pathetic turns, will be found the best reading by girls of all ages, and by boys too.*"—TIMES.
SYBIL'S BOOK. Illustrated by S. E. WALLER. Second Edition. Globe 8vo. gilt. 4s. 6d.
"*Another of Lady Barker's delightful stories, and one of the most thoroughly original books for girls that has been written for many years. Grown-up readers will like it quite as much as young people, and will even better understand the rarity of such simple, natural, and unaffected writing . . . . That no one can read the story without interest is not its highest praise, for no one ought to be able to lay it down without being the better girl or boy, or man or woman, for the reading of it. Lady Barker has never turned her fertile and fascinating pen to better account, and for the sake of all readers we wish 'Sybil's Book's a wide success.*"—TIMES.

Bell.—ROMANCES AND MINOR POEMS. By HENRY GLASSFORD BELL. Fcap. 8vo. 6s.

"*Full of life and genius.*"—COURT CIRCULAR.

Besant.—STUDIES IN EARLY FRENCH POETRY. By WALTER BESANT, M.A. Crown 8vo. 8s. 6d.

The present work aims to afford information and direction touching the early efforts of France in poetical literature. "*In one moderately sized volume he has contrived to introduce us to the very best, if not to all of the early French poets.*"—ATHENÆUM.

Betsy Lee; A FO'C'S'LE YARN. Extra fcap. 8vo. 3s. 6d.

"*There is great vigour and much pathos in this poem.*"—MORNING POST.

"*We can at least say that it is the work of a true poet.*"—ATHENÆUM.

Black (W.)—Works by W. BLACK, Author of "A Daughter of Heth."

THE STRANGE ADVENTURES OF A PHAETON. Seventh and Cheaper Edition. Crown 8vo. 6s. Also, Illustrated by S. E. WALLER, 8vo. cloth gilt. 10s. 6d.

"*The book is a really charming description of a thousand English landscapes and of the emergencies and the fun and the delight of a picnic journey through them by a party determined to enjoy themselves, and as well matched as the pair of horses which drew the phaeton they sat in. The real charm and purpose of the book is its open-air life among hills and dales.*"—TIMES. "*The great charm of Mr. Black's book is that there is nothing hackneyed about it, nothing overdrawn,—all is bright and lifelike.*"—MORNING POST.

A PRINCESS OF THULE. Three vols. Sixth and cheaper Edition. Crown 8vo. 6s.

The SATURDAY REVIEW says:—"*A novel which is both romantic and natural, which has much feeling, without any touch of mawkishness, which goes deep into character without any suggestion of painful analysis—this is a rare gem to find amongst the débris of current literature, and this, or nearly this, Mr. Black has given us in the 'Princess of Thule.'*" "*It has, for one thing, the great charm of novelty. . . . There is a picturesqueness in all that Mr. Black writes, but scarcely even in the 'Adventures of a Phaeton' are there the freshness and sweetness and perfect sense of natural beauty we find in this last book.*"—PALL MALL GAZETTE. "*A beautiful and nearly perfect story.*"—SPECTATOR.

Borland Hall.—By the Author of "Olrig Grange." Crown 8vo. 7s.

Brooke.—THE FOOL OF QUALITY; OR, THE HISTORY OF HENRY, EARL OF MORELAND. By HENRY BROOKE. Newly revised, with a Biographical Preface by the Rev. CHARLES KINGSLEY, M.A., Rector of Eversley. Crown 8vo. 6s.

BELLES LETTRES.

Broome.—THE STRANGER OF SERIPHOS. A Dramatic Poem. By FREDERICK NAPIER BROOME. Fcap. 8vo. 5s.
Founded on the Greek legend of Danaë and Perseus. "*Grace and beauty of expression are Mr. Broome's characteristics; and these qualities are displayed in many passages.*"—ATHENÆUM. "*The story is rendered with consummate beauty.*"—LITERARY CHURCHMAN.

Buist.—BIRDS, THEIR CAGES AND THEIR KEEP: Being a Practical Manual of Bird-Keeping and Bird-Rearing. By K. A. BUIST. With Coloured Frontispiece and other Illustrations. Crown 8vo. 5s.

Burnand.—MY TIME, AND WHAT I'VE DONE WITH IT. By F. C. BURNAND. Crown 8vo. 6s.

Cabinet Pictures.—Oblong folio, price 42s.
CONTENTS:—"*Childe Harold's Pilgrimage*" and "*The Fighting Téméraire,*" by J. M. W. Turner; "*Crossing the Bridge,*" by Sir W. A. Callcott; "*The Cornfield,*" by John Constable; and "*A Landscape,*" by Birket Foster. The DAILY NEWS says of them, "*They are very beautifully executed, and might be framed and hung up on the wall, as creditable substitutes for the originals.*"

CABINET PICTURES. A Second Series.
Containing:—"*The Baths of Caligula*" and "*The Golden Bough,*" by J. W. M. Turner; "*The Little Brigand,*" by T. Uwins; "*The Lake of Lucerne,*" by Percival Skelton; "*Evening Rest,*" by E. M. Wimperis. Oblong folio. 42s.

Carroll.—Works by "LEWIS CARROLL:"—
ALICE'S ADVENTURES IN WONDERLAND. With Forty-two Illustrations by TENNIEL. 46th Thousand. Crown 8vo. cloth. 6s.
A GERMAN TRANSLATION OF THE SAME. With TENNIEL'S Illustrations. Crown 8vo. gilt. 6s.
A FRENCH TRANSLATION OF THE SAME. With TENNIEL'S Illustrations. Crown 8vo. gilt. 6s.
AN ITALIAN TRANSLATION OF THE SAME. By T. P. ROSSETTE. With TENNIEL'S Illustrations. Crown 8vo. 6s.
"*Beyond question supreme among modern books for children.*"—SPECTATOR. "*One of the choicest and most charming books ever composed for a child's reading.*"—PALL MALL GAZETTE. "*A very pretty and highly original book, sure to delight the little world of wondering minds, and which may well please those who have unfortunately passed the years of wondering.*"—TIMES.

THROUGH THE LOOKING-GLASS, AND WHAT ALICE FOUND THERE. With Fifty Illustrations by TENNIEL. Crown 8vo. gilt. 6s. 35th Thousand.
"*Quite as rich in humorous whims of fantasy, quite as laughable*

in its queer incidents, as loveable for its pleasant spirit and graceful manner, as the wondrous tale of Alice's former adventures."—ILLUSTRATED LONDON NEWS. "*If this had been given to the world first it would have enjoyed a success at least equal to ' Alice in Wonderland.'*"—STANDARD.

Children's (The) Garland, FROM THE BEST POETS. Selected and arranged by COVENTRY PATMORE. New Edition. With Illustrations by J. LAWSON. Crown 8vo. Cloth extra. 6s.

Christmas Carol (A). Printed in Colours from Original Designs by Mr. and Mrs. TREVOR CRISPIN, with Illuminated Borders from MSS. of the 14th and 15th Centuries. Imp. 4to. cloth inlaid, gilt edges, £3 3s. Also a Cheaper Edition, 21s.
"*A most exquisitely got up volume. Legend, carol, and text are preciously enshrined in its emblazoned pages, and the illuminated borders are far and away the best example of their art we have seen this Christmas. The pictures and borders are harmonious in their colouring, the dyes are brilliant without being raw, and the volume is a trophy of colour-printing. The binding by Burn is in the very best taste.*"—TIMES.

Church (A. J.)—HORÆ TENNYSONIANÆ, Sive Eclogæ e Tennysono Latine redditæ. Curâ A. J. CHURCH, A.M. Extra fcap. 8vo. 6s.
"*Of Mr. Church's ode we may speak in almost unqualified praise, and the same may be said of the contributions generally.*"—PALL MALL GAZETTE.

Clough (Arthur Hugh).—THE POEMS AND PROSE REMAINS OF ARTHUR HUGH CLOUGH. With a Selection from his Letters and a Memoir. Edited by his Wife. With Portrait. Two Vols. Crown 8vo. 21s.
"*Taken as a whole,*" the SPECTATOR says, "*these volumes cannot fail to be a lasting monument of one of the most original men of our age.*" "*Full of charming letters from Rome,*" says the MORNING STAR, "*from Greece, from America, from Oxford, and from Rugby.*"

THE POEMS OF ARTHUR HUGH CLOUGH, sometime Fellow of Oriel College, Oxford. Fourth Edition. Fcap. 8vo. 6s.
"*From the higher mind of cultivated, all-questioning, but still conservative England, in this our puzzled generation, we do not know of any utterance in literature so characteristic as the poems of Arthur Hugh Clough.*"—FRASER'S MAGAZINE.

Clunes.—THE STORY OF PAULINE: an Autobiography. By G. C. CLUNES. Crown 8vo. 6s.
"*Both for vivid delineation of character and fluent lucidity of style, ' The Story of Pauline' is in the first rank of modern fiction.*"—GLOBE. "*Told with delightful vivacity, thorough appreciation of life, and a complete knowledge of character.*"—MANCHESTER EXAMINER.

BELLES LETTRES.

Collects of the Church of England. With a beautifully Coloured Floral Design to each Collect, and Illuminated Cover. Crown 8vo. 12s. Also kept in various styles of morocco.

"*This is beyond question,*" *the* ART JOURNAL *says,* "*the most beautiful book of the season.*" *The* GUARDIAN *thinks it* "*a successful attempt to associate in a natural and unforced manner the flowers of our fields and gardens with the course of the Christian year.*"

Cox.—RECOLLECTIONS OF OXFORD. By G. V. COX, M.A., late Esquire Bedel and Coroner in the University of Oxford. Second and cheaper Edition. Crown 8vo. 6s.

The TIMES *says that it* "*will pleasantly recall in many a country parsonage the memory of youthful days.*"

Culmshire Folk.—By IGNOTUS. Three vols. Crown 8vo. 31s. 6d.

"*Its sparkling pleasantness, its drollery, its shrewdness, the charming little bits of character which frequently come in, its easy liveliness, and a certain chattiness which, while it is never vulgar, brings the writer very near, and makes one feel as if the story were being told in lazy confidence in an hour of idleness by a man who, while thoroughly good-natured, is strongly humorous, and has an ever-present perception of the absurdities of people and things.*"—SPECTATOR.

Dante.—DANTE'S COMEDY, THE HELL. Translated by W. M. ROSSETTI. Fcap. 8vo. cloth. 5s.

"*The aim of this translation of Dante may be summed up in one word—Literality. To follow Dante sentence for sentence, line for line, word for word—neither more nor less, has been my strenuous endeavour.*"—AUTHOR'S PREFACE.

Days of Old; STORIES FROM OLD ENGLISH HISTORY. By the Author of "Ruth and her Friends." New Edition. 18mo. cloth, extra. 2s. 6d.

"*Full of truthful and charming historic pictures, is everywhere vital with moral and religious principles, and is written with a brightness of description, and with a dramatic force in the representation of character, that have made, and will always make, it one of the greatest favourites with reading boys.*"—NONCONFORMIST.

Deane.—MARJORY. By MILLY DEANE. Third Edition. With Frontispiece and Vignette. Crown 8vo. 4s. 6d.

The TIMES *of September 11th says it is* "*A very touching story, full of promise for the after career of the authoress. It is so tenderly drawn, and so full of life and grace, that any attempt to analyse or describe it falls sadly short of the original. We will venture to say that few readers of any natural feeling or sensibility will take up 'Marjory' without reading it through at a sitting, and we hope we shall see more stories by the same hand.*" *The* MORNING POST *calls it* "*A deliciously fresh and charming little love story.*"

De Vere.—THE INFANT BRIDAL, and other Poems. By AUBREY DE VERE. Fcap. 8vo. 7s. 6d.

"*Mr. De Vere has taken his place among the poets of the day. Pure and tender feeling, and that polished restraint of style which is called classical, are the charms of the volume.*"—SPECTATOR.

Doyle (Sir F. H.)—LECTURES ON POETRY, delivered before the University of Oxford in 1868. By Sir FRANCIS HASTINGS DOYLE, Professor of Poetry in the University of Oxford. Crown 8vo. 3*s*. 6*d*.
"*Full of thoughtful discrimination and fine insight: the lecture on 'Provincial Poetry' seems to us singularly true, eloquent, and instructive.*"—SPECTATOR.

Estelle Russell.—By the Author of "The Private Life of Galileo." New Edition. Crown 8vo. 6*s*.
Full of bright pictures of French life. The English family, whose fortunes form the main drift of the story, reside mostly in France, but there are also many English characters and scenes of great interest. It is certainly the work of a fresh, vigorous, and most interesting writer, with a dash of sarcastic humour which is refreshing and not too bitter. "We can send our readers to it with confidence."
—SPECTATOR.

Evans.—BROTHER FABIAN'S MANUSCRIPT, AND OTHER POEMS. By SEBASTIAN EVANS. Fcap. 8vo. cloth. 6*s*.
"*In this volume we have full assurance that he has 'the vision and the faculty divine.' . . . Clever and full of kindly humour.*"—GLOBE.

Evans.—THE CURSE OF IMMORTALITY. By A. EUBULE EVANS. Crown 8vo. 6*s*.
"*Never, probably, has the legend of the Wandering Jew been more ably and poetically handled. The author writes as a true poet, and with the skill of a true artist. The plot of this remarkable drama is not only well contrived, but worked out with a degree of simplicity and truthful vigour altogether unusual in modern poetry. In fact, since the date of Byron's 'Cain,' we can scarcely recall any verse at once so terse, so powerful, and so masterly.*"—STANDARD.

Fairy Book.—The Best Popular Fairy Stories. Selected and Rendered anew by the Author of "John Halifax, Gentleman." With Coloured Illustrations and Ornamental Borders by J. E. ROGERS, Author of "Ridicula Rediviva." Crown 8vo. cloth, extra gilt. 6*s*. (Golden Treasury Edition. 18mo. 4*s*. 6*d*.)
"*A delightful selection, in a delightful external form.*"—SPECTATOR.
"*A book which will prove delightful to children all the year round.*"
—PALL MALL GAZETTE.

Fletcher.—THOUGHTS FROM A GIRL'S LIFE. By LUCY FLETCHER. Second Edition. Fcap. 8vo. 4*s*. 6*d*.
"*The poems are all graceful; they are marked throughout by an accent of reality; the thoughts and emotions are genuine.*"—ATHENÆUM.

Garnett.—IDYLLS AND EPIGRAMS. Chiefly from the Greek Anthology. By RICHARD GARNETT. Fcap. 8vo. 2*s*. 6*d*.
"*A charming little book. For English readers, Mr. Garnett's*

BELLES LETTRES.

translations will open a new world of thought."—WESTMINSTER REVIEW.

Gilmore.—STORM WARRIORS; OR, LIFE-BOAT WORK ON THE GOODWIN SANDS. By the Rev. JOHN GILMORE, M.A., Rector of Holy Trinity, Ramsgate, Author of "The Ramsgate Life-Boat," in *Macmillan's Magazine.* Crown 8vo. 6s.
"*The stories, which are said to be literally exact, are more thrilling than anything in fiction. Mr. Gilmore has done a good work as well as written a good book.*"—DAILY NEWS.

Gladstone.—JUVENTUS MUNDI. The Gods and Men of the Heroic Age. By the Right Hon. W. E. GLADSTONE, M.P. Crown 8vo. cloth extra. With Map. 10s. 6d. Second Edition.
"*To read these brilliant details,*" *says the* ATHENÆUM, "*is like standing on the Olympian threshold and gazing at the ineffable brightness within.*" *According to the* WESTMINSTER REVIEW, "*it would be difficult to point out a book that contains so much fulness of knowledge along with so much freshness of perception and clearness of presentation.*"

Gray.—THE POETICAL WORKS OF DAVID GRAY. New and Enlarged Edition. Edited by HENRY GLASSFORD BELL, late Sheriff of Lanarkshire. Crown 8vo. 6s.

Guesses at Truth.—By TWO BROTHERS. With Vignette Title and Frontispiece. New Edition, with Memoir. Fcap. 8vo. 6s. Also see Golden Treasury Series.

Halifax.—AFTER LONG YEARS. By M. C. HALIFAX. Crown 8vo. 10s. 6d.
"*A story of very unusual merit. The entire story is well conceived, well written, and well carried out; and the reader will look forward with pleasure to meeting this clever author again.*"—DAILY NEWS. "*This is a very pretty, simple love story..... The author possesses a very graceful, womanly pen, and tells the story with a rare tender simplicity which well befits it.*"—STANDARD.

Hamerton.—A PAINTER'S CAMP. Second Edition, revised. Extra fcap. 8vo. 6s.
BOOK I. *In England;* BOOK II. *In Scotland;* BOOK III. *In France.*
"*These pages, written with infinite spirit and humour, bring into close rooms, back upon tired heads, the breezy airs of Lancashire moors and Highland lochs, with a freshness which no recent novelist has succeeded in preserving.*"—NONCONFORMIST.

Heaton.—HAPPY SPRING TIME. Illustrated by OSCAR PLETSCH. With Rhymes for Mothers and Children. By MRS. CHARLES HEATON. Crown 8vo. cloth extra, gilt edges. 3s. 6d.
"*The pictures in this book are capital.*"—ATHENÆUM.

Hervey.—DUKE ERNEST, a Tragedy; and other Poems. Fcap. 8vo. 6s.
"*Conceived in pure taste and true historic feeling, and presented with*

BELLES LETTRES.

much dramatic force. . . . Thoroughly original."—BRITISH QUARTERLY.

Higginson.—MALBONE: An Oldport Romance. By T. W. HIGGINSON. Fcap. 8vo. 2s. 6d.

The DAILY NEWS says: *"Who likes a quiet story, full of mature thought, of clear, humorous surprises, of artistic studious design? 'Malbone' is a rare work, possessing these characteristics, and replete, too, with honest literary effort."*

Hillside Rhymes.—Extra fcap. 8vo. 5s.

Home.—BLANCHE LISLE, and other Poems. By CECIL HOME. Fcap. 8vo. 4s. 6d.

Hood (Tom).—THE PLEASANT TALE OF PUSS AND ROBIN AND THEIR FRIENDS, KITTY AND BOB. Told in Pictures by L. FRÖLICH, and in Rhymes by TOM HOOD. Crown 8vo. gilt. 3s. 6d.

"The volume is prettily got up, and is sure to be a favourite in the nursery."—SCOTSMAN. *"Herr Frölich has outdone himself in his pictures of this dramatic chase."*—MORNING POST.

Keary (A.)—Works by Miss A. KEARY:—

JANET'S HOME. New Edition. Globe 8vo. 2s. 6d.

"Never did a more charming family appear upon the canvas; and most skilfully and felicitously have their characters been portrayed. Each individual of the fireside is a finished portrait, distinct and lifelike. . . . The future before her as a novelist is that of becoming the Miss Austin of her generation."—SUN.

CLEMENCY FRANKLYN. New Edition. Globe 8vo. 2s. 6d.

"Full of wisdom and goodness, simple, truthful, and artistic. . . It is capital as a story; better still in its pure tone and wholesome influence."—GLOBE.

OLDBURY. Three vols. Crown 8vo. 31s. 6d.

"This is a very powerfully written story."—GLOBE. *"This is a really excellent novel."*—ILLUSTRATED LONDON NEWS. *"The sketches of society in Oldbury are excellent. The pictures of child life are full of truth."*—WESTMINSTER REVIEW.

Keary (A. and E.)—Works by A. and E. KEARY:—

THE LITTLE WANDERLIN, and other Fairy Tales. 18mo. 2s. 6d.

"The tales are fanciful and well written, and they are sure to win favour amongst little readers."—ATHENÆUM.

THE HEROES OF ASGARD. Tales from Scandinavian Mythology. New and Revised Edition, Illustrated by HUARD. Extra fcap. 8vo. 4s. 6d.

"Told in a light and amusing style, which, in its drollery and quaintness, reminds us of our old favourite Grimm."—TIMES.

Kingsley.—Works by the Rev. CHARLES KINGSLEY, M.A., Rector of Eversley, and Canon of Westminster :—

"WESTWARD HO!" or, The Voyages and Adventures of Sir Amyas Leigh. Ninth Edition. Crown 8vo. 6s.

Kingsley (C.)—*continued.*

FRASER'S MAGAZINE *calls it "almost the best historical novel of the day."*

TWO YEARS AGO. Fifth Edition. Crown 8vo. 6s.

"*Mr. Kingsley has provided us all along with such pleasant diversions—such rich and brightly tinted glimpses of natural history, such suggestive remarks on mankind, society, and all sorts of topics, that amidst the pleasure of the way, the circuit to be made will be by most forgotten.*"—GUARDIAN.

HYPATIA; or, New Foes with an Old Face. Seventh Edition. Crown 8vo. 6s.

HEREWARD THE WAKE—LAST OF THE ENGLISH. Second Edition. Crown 8vo. 6s.

YEAST: A Problem. Sixth Edition. Crown 8vo. 5s.

ALTON LOCKE. New Edition. With a New Preface. Crown 8vo. 4s. 6d.

The author shows, to quote the SPECTATOR, "*what it is that constitutes the true Christian, God-fearing, man-living gentleman.*"

THE WATER BABIES. A Fairy Tale for a Land Baby. New Edition, with additional Illustrations by Sir NOEL PATON, R.S.A., and P. SKELTON. Crown 8vo. cloth, extra gilt. 5s.

"*In fun, in humour, and in innocent imagination, as a child's book we do not know its equal.*"—LONDON REVIEW. "*Mr. Kingsley must have the credit of revealing to us a new order of life. . . . There is in the 'Water Babies' an abundance of wit, fun, good humour, geniality, élan, go.*"—TIMES.

THE HEROES; or, Greek Fairy Tales for my Children. With Coloured Illustrations. New Edition. 18mo. 4s. 6d.

"*We do not think these heroic stories have ever been more attractively told. . . There is a deep under-current of religious feeling traceable throughout its pages which is sure to influence young readers powerfully.*"—LONDON REVIEW. "*One of the children's books that will surely become a classic.*"—NONCONFORMIST.

PHAETHON; or, Loose Thoughts for Loose Thinkers. Third Edition. Crown 8vo. 2s.

"*The dialogue of 'Phaethon' has striking beauties, and its suggestions may meet half-way many a latent doubt, and, like a light breeze, lift from the soul clouds that are gathering heavily, and threatening to settle down in misty gloom on the summer of many a fair and promising young life.*"—SPECTATOR.

POEMS; including The Saint's Tragedy, Andromeda, Songs, Ballads, etc. Complete Collected Edition. Extra fcap. 8vo. 6s. The SPECTATOR *calls "Andromeda" "the finest piece of English hexameter verse that has ever been written. It is a volume which many readers will be glad to possess."*

PROSE IDYLLS. NEW AND OLD. Second Edition. Crown 8vo. 5s.

CONTENTS :—*A Charm of Birds; Chalk-Stream Studies; The Fens; My Winter-Garden; From Ocean to Sea; North Devon.*

"*Altogether a delightful book. . . . It exhibits the author's best traits, and cannot fail to infect the reader with a love of nature and of out-door life and its enjoyments. It is well calculated to bring a gleam of summer with its pleasant associations, into the bleak winter-time; while a better companion for a summer ramble could hardly be found.*"—BRITISH QUARTERLY REVIEW.

Kingsley (H.)—Works by HENRY KINGSLEY :—
TALES OF OLD TRAVEL. Re-narrated. With Eight full-page Illustrations by HUARD. Fourth Edition. Crown 8vo. cloth, extra gilt. 5s.
"*We know no better book for those who want knowledge or seek to refresh it. As for the 'sensational,' most novels are tame compared with these narratives.*"—ATHENÆUM. "*Exactly the book to interest and to do good to intelligent and high-spirited boys.*"—LITERARY CHURCHMAN.

THE LOST CHILD. With Eight Illustrations by FRÖLICH. Crown 4to. cloth gilt. 3s. 6d.
"*A pathetic story, and told so as to give children an interest in Australian ways and scenery.*"—GLOBE. "*Very charmingly and very touchingly told.*"—SATURDAY REVIEW.

OAKSHOTT CASTLE. 3 Vols. Crown 8vo. 31s. 6d.
"*No one who takes up 'Oakshott Castle' will willingly put it down until the last page is turned. . . . It may fairly be considered a capital story, full of go, and abounding in word pictures of storms and wrecks.*"—OBSERVER.

Knatchbull-Hugessen.—Works by E. H. KNATCHBULL-HUGESSEN, M.P. :—
Mr. *Knatchbull-Hugessen has won for himself a reputation as a teller of fairy-tales.* "*His powers,*" *says the* TIMES, "*are of a very high order; light and brilliant narrative flows from his pen, and is fed by an invention as graceful as it is inexhaustible.*" "*Children reading his stories,*" *the* SCOTSMAN *says*, "*or hearing them read, will have their minds refreshed and invigorated as much as their bodies would be by abundance of fresh air and exercise.*"

STORIES FOR MY CHILDREN. With Illustrations. Fourth Edition. Crown 8vo. 5s.
"*The stories are charming, and full of life and fun.*"—STANDARD.
"*The author has an imagination as fanciful as Grimm himself, while some of his stories are superior to anything that Hans Christian Andersen has written.*"—NONCONFORMIST.

CRACKERS FOR CHRISTMAS. More Stories. With Illustrations by JELLICOE and ELWES. Fourth Edition. Crown 8vo. 5s.
"*A fascinating little volume, which will make him friends in every household in which there are children.*"—DAILY NEWS.

MOONSHINE : Fairy Tales. With Illustrations by W. BRUNTON. Sixth Edition. Crown 8vo. cloth gilt. 5s.
"*A volume of fairy tales, written not only for ungrown children,*

BELLES LETTRES.

Knatchbull-Hugessen (E. H.)—*continued.*
but for bigger, and if you are nearly worn out, or sick, or sorry, you will find it good reading."—GRAPHIC. *"The most charming volume of fairy tales which we have ever read.... We cannot quit this very pleasant book without a word of praise to its illustrator, Mr. Brunton from first to last has done admirably."*—TIMES.

TALES AT TEA-TIME. Fairy Stories. With Seven Illustrations by W. BRUNTON. Fifth Edition. Crown 8vo. cloth gilt. 5s.
"Capitally illustrated by W. Brunton.... In frolic and fancy they are quite equal to his other books. The author knows how to write fairy stories as they should be written. The whole book is full of the most delightful drolleries."—TIMES.

QUEER FOLK. FAIRY STORIES. Illustrated by S. E. WALLER. Fourth Edition. Crown 8vo. Cloth gilt. 5s.
"Decidedly the author's happiest effort.... One of the best story books of the year."—HOUR.

Knatchbull-Hugessen (Louisa).—THE HISTORY OF PRINCE PERRYPETS. A Fairy Tale. By LOUISA KNATCHBULL-HUGESSEN. With Eight Illustrations by WEIGAND. New Edition. Crown 4to. cloth gilt. 3s. 6d.
"A grand and exciting fairy tale."—MORNING POST. *"A delicious piece of fairy nonsense."*—ILLUSTRATED LONDON NEWS.

Knox.—SONGS OF CONSOLATION. By ISA CRAIG KNOX. Extra fcap. 8vo. Cloth extra, gilt edges. 4s. 6d.
"The verses are truly sweet; there is in them not only much genuine poetic quality, but an ardent, flowing devotedness, and a peculiar skill in propounding theological tenets in the most graceful way, which any divine might envy."—SCOTSMAN.

Latham.—SERTUM SHAKSPERIANUM, Subnexis aliquot aliunde excerptis floribus. Latine reddidit Rev. H. LATHAM, M.A. Extra fcap. 8vo. 5s.

Lemon.—THE LEGENDS OF NUMBER NIP. By MARK LEMON. With Illustrations by C. KEENE. New Edition. Extra fcap. 8vo. 2s. 6d.

Life and Times of Conrad the Squirrel. A Story for Children. By the Author of "Wandering Willie," "Effie's Friends," &c. With a Frontispiece by R. FARREN. Second Edition. Crown 8vo. 3s. 6d.
"Having commenced on the first page, we were compelled to go on to the conclusion, and this we predict will be the case with every one who opens the book."—PALL MALL GAZETTE.

Little Estella, and other FAIRY TALES FOR THE YOUNG. 18mo. cloth extra. 2s. 6d.
"This is a fine story, and we thank heaven for not being too wise to enjoy it."—DAILY NEWS.

Lowell.—Works by J. Russell LOWELL:—
AMONG MY BOOKS. Six Essays. Dryden — Witchcraft —

Lowell—*continued.*
Shakespeare once More—New England Two Centuries Ago—Lessing—Rousseau and the Sentimentalists. Crown 8vo. 7s. 6d.
"*We may safely say the volume is one of which our chief complaint must be that there is not more of it. There are good sense and lively feeling forcibly and tersely expressed in every page of his writing.*"—PALL MALL GAZETTE.

COMPLETE POETICAL WORKS of JAMES RUSSELL LOWELL. With Portrait, engraved by Jeens. 18mo. cloth extra. 4s. 6d.
"*All readers who are able to recognise and appreciate genuine verse will give a glad welcome to this beautiful little volume.*"—PALL MALL GAZETTE.

Lyttelton.—Works by LORD LYTTELTON :—
THE "COMUS" OF MILTON, rendered into Greek Verse. Extra fcap. 8vo. 5s.
THE "SAMSON AGONISTES" OF MILTON, rendered into Greek Verse. Extra fcap. 8vo. 6s. 6d.
"*Classical in spirit, full of force, and true to the original.*"—GUARDIAN.

Maclaren.—THE FAIRY FAMILY. A series of Ballads and Metrical Tales illustrating the Fairy Mythology of Europe. By ARCHIBALD MACLAREN. With Frontispiece, Illustrated Title, and Vignette. Crown 8vo. gilt. 5s.
"*A successful attempt to translate into the vernacular some of the Fairy Mythology of Europe. The verses are very good. There is no shirking difficulties of rhyme, and the ballad metre which is oftenest employed has a great deal of the kind of 'go' which we find so seldom outside the pages of Scott. The book is of permanent value.*"—GUARDIAN.

Macmillan's Magazine.—Published Monthly. Price 1s. Volumes I. to XXIX. are now ready. 7s. 6d. each.

Macquoid.—PATTY. By KATHARINE S. MACQUOID. Third and Cheaper Edition. Crown 8vo. 6s.
"*A book to be read.*"—STANDARD. "*A powerful and fascinating story.*"—DAILY TELEGRAPH. *The* GLOBE *considers it "well-written, amusing, and interesting, and has the merit of being out of the ordinary run of novels.*"

Maguire.—YOUNG PRINCE MARIGOLD, AND OTHER FAIRY STORIES. By the late JOHN FRANCIS MAGUIRE, M.P. Illustrated by S. E. WALLER. Globe 8vo. gilt. 4s. 6d.
"*The author has evidently studied the ways and tastes of children and got at the secret of amusing them; and has succeeded in what is not so easy a task as it may seem—in producing a really good children's book.*"—DAILY TELEGRAPH.

Marlitt (E.)—THE COUNTESS GISELA. Translated from the German of E. MARLITT. Crown 8vo. 7s. 6d.
"*A very beautiful story of German country life.*"—LITERARY CHURCHMAN.

BELLES LETTRES.

Masson (Professor).—Works by DAVID MASSON, M.A., Professor of Rhetoric and English Literature in the University of Edinburgh.
BRITISH NOVELISTS AND THEIR STYLES. Being a Critical Sketch of the History of British Prose Fiction. Crown 8vo. 7s. 6d.
WORDSWORTH, SHELLEY, KEATS, AND OTHER ESSAYS. Crown 8vo. 5s.
CHATTERTON: A Story of the Year 1770. Crown 8vo. 5s.
THE THREE DEVILS: LUTHER'S, MILTON'S, and GOETHE'S; and other Essays. Crown 8vo. 5s.

Mazini.—IN THE GOLDEN SHELL; A Story of Palermo. By LINDA MAZINI. With Illustrations. Globe 8vo. cloth gilt. 4s. 6d.

"*As beautiful and bright and fresh as the scenes to which it wafts us over the blue Mediterranean, and as pure and innocent, but piquant and sprightly as the little girl who plays the part of its heroine, is this admirable little book.*"—ILLUSTRATED LONDON NEWS.

Merivale.—KEATS' HYPERION, rendered into Latin Verse. By C. MERIVALE, B.D. Second Edition. Extra fcap. 8vo. 3s. 6d.

Milner.—THE LILY OF LUMLEY. By EDITH MILNER. Crown 8vo. 7s. 6d.

"*The novel is a good one and decidedly worth the reading.*"—EXAMINER. "*A pretty, brightly-written story.*"—LITERARY CHURCHMAN. "*A tale possessing the deepest interest.*"—COURT JOURNAL.

Milton's Poetical Works.—Edited with Text collated from the best Authorities, with Introduction and Notes by DAVID MASSON. Three vols. 8vo. With Three Portraits engraved by C. H. JEENS and RADCLIFFE. (Uniform with the Cambridge Shakespeare.)

Mistral (F.)—MIRELLE, a Pastoral Epic of Provence. Translated by H. CRICHTON. Extra fcap. 8vo. 6s.

"*It would be hard to overpraise the sweetness and pleasing freshness of this charming epic.*"—ATHENÆUM. "*A good translation of a poem that deserves to be known by all students of literature and friends of old-world simplicity in story-telling.*"—NONCONFORMIST.

Mitford (A. B.)—TALES OF OLD JAPAN. By A. B. MITFORD, Second Secretary to the British Legation in Japan. With Illustrations drawn and cut on Wood by Japanese Artists. New and Cheaper Edition. Crown 8vo. 6s.

"*They will always be interesting as memorials of a most exceptional society; while, regarded simply as tales, they are sparkling, sensational, and dramatic, and the originality of their ideas and the quaintness of their language give them a most captivating piquancy.*"

The illustrations are extremely interesting, and for the curious in such matters have a special and particular value."—PALL MALL GAZETTE.

Mr. Pisistratus Brown, M.P., IN THE HIGHLANDS. New Edition, with Illustrations. Crown 8vo. 3s. 6d.

"*The book is calculated to recall pleasant memories of holidays well spent, and scenes not easily to be forgotten. To those who have never been in the Western Highlands, or sailed along the Frith of Clyde and on the Western Coast, it will seem almost like a fairy story. There is a charm in the volume which makes it anything but easy for a reader who has opened it to put it down until the last page has been read.*"—SCOTSMAN.

Mrs. Jerningham's Journal. A Poem purporting to be the Journal of a newly-married Lady. Second Edition. Fcap. 8vo. 3s. 6d.

"*It is nearly a perfect gem. We have had nothing so good for a long time, and those who neglect to read it are neglecting one of the jewels of contemporary history.*"—EDINBURGH DAILY REVIEW. "*One quality in the piece, sufficient of itself to claim a moment's attention, is that it is unique—original, indeed, is not too strong a word—in the manner of its conception and execution.*" —PALL MALL GAZETTE.

Mudie.—STRAY LEAVES. By C. E. MUDIE. New Edition. Extra fcap. 8vo. 3s. 6d. Contents:—"His and Mine"— "Night and Day"—"One of Many," &c.

This little volume consists of a number of poems, mostly of a genuinely devotional character. "They are for the most part so exquisitely sweet and delicate as to be quite a marvel of composition. They are worthy of being laid up in the recesses of the heart, and recalled to memory from time to time."—ILLUSTRATED LONDON NEWS.

Murray.—THE BALLADS AND SONGS OF SCOTLAND, in View of their Influence on the Character of the People. By J. CLARK MURRAY, LL.D., Professor of Mental and Moral Philosophy in McGill College, Montreal. Crown 8vo. 6s.

"*Independently of the lucidity of the style in which the whole book is written, the selection of the examples alone would recommend it to favour, while the geniality of the criticism upon those examples cannot fail to make them highly appreciated and valued.*"— MORNING POST.

Myers (Ernest).—THE PURITANS. By ERNEST MYERS. Extra fcap. 8vo. cloth. 2s. 6d.

"*It is not too much to call it a really grand poem, stately and dignified, and showing not only a high poetic mind, but also great power over poetic expression.*"—LITERARY CHURCHMAN.

Myers (F. W. H.)—POEMS. By F. W. H. MYERS. Containing "St. Paul," "St. John," and others. Extra fcap. 8vo. 4s. 6d.

"*It is rare to find a writer who combines to such an extent the faculty*

BELLES LETTRES.

of communicating feelings with the faculty of euphonious expression."—SPECTATOR. *"'St. Paul' stands without a rival as the noblest religious poem which has been written in an age which beyond any other has been prolific in this class of poetry. The sublimest conceptions are expressed in language which, for richness, taste, and purity, we have never seen excelled."*—JOHN BULL.

Nichol.—HANNIBAL, A HISTORICAL DRAMA. By JOHN NICHOL, B.A. Oxon., Regius Professor of English Language and Literature in the University of Glasgow. Extra fcap. 8vo. 7s. 6d.
"The poem combines in no ordinary degree firmness and workmanship. After the lapse of many centuries, an English poet is found paying to the great Carthagenian the worthiest poetical tribute which has as yet, to our knowledge, been afforded to his noble and stainless name."—SATURDAY REVIEW.

Nine Years Old.—By the Author of "St. Olave's," "When I was a Little Girl," &c. Illustrated by FRÖLICH. Third Edition. Extra fcap. 8vo. cloth gilt. 4s. 6d.
It is believed that this story, by the favourably known author of "St. Olave's," will be found both highly interesting and instructive to the young. The volume contains eight graphic illustrations by Mr. L. Frölich. The EXAMINER *says: "Whether the readers are nine years old, or twice, or seven times as old, they must enjoy this pretty volume."*

Noel.—BEATRICE, AND OTHER POEMS. By the Hon. RODEN NOEL. Fcap. 8vo. 6s.
"It is impossible to read the poem through without being powerfully moved. There are passages in it which for intensity and tenderness, clear and vivid vision, spontaneous and delicate sympathy, may be compared with the best efforts of our best living writers."—SPECTATOR.

Norton.—Works by the Hon. Mrs. NORTON :—

THE LADY OF LA GARAYE. With Vignette and Frontispiece. New Edition. Fcap. 8vo. 4s. 6d.
"Full of thought well expressed, and may be classed among her best efforts."—TIMES.

OLD SIR DOUGLAS. Cheap Edition. Globe 8vo. 2s. 6d.
"This varied and lively novel—this clever novel so full of character, and of fine incidental remark."—SCOTSMAN. *"One of the pleasantest and healthiest stories of modern fiction."*—GLOBE.

Oliphant.—Works by Mrs. OLIPHANT :—

AGNES HOPETOUN'S SCHOOLS AND HOLIDAYS. New Edition with Illustrations. Royal 16mo. gilt leaves. 4s. 6d.
"There are few books of late years more fitted to touch the heart, purify the feeling, and quicken and sustain right principles."—NONCONFORMIST. *"A more gracefully written story it is impossible to desire."*—DAILY NEWS.

A SON OF THE SOIL. New Edition. Globe 8vo. 2s. 6d.
"It is a very different work from the ordinary run of novels.

BELLES LETTRES.

The whole life of a man is portrayed in it, worked out with subtlety and insight."—ATHENÆUM.

Our Year. A Child's Book, in Prose and Verse. By the Author of "John Halifax, Gentleman." Illustrated by CLARENCE DOBELL. Royal 16mo. 3s. 6d.
"*It is just the book we could wish to see in the hands of every child.*"—ENGLISH CHURCHMAN.

Olrig Grange. Edited by HERMANN KUNST, Philol. Professor. Extra fcap. 8vo. 6s. 6d.
"*A masterly and original power of impression, pouring itself forth in clear, sweet, strong rhythm.... It is a fine poem, full of life, of music and of clear vision.*"—NORTH BRITISH DAILY MAIL.

Oxford Spectator, The.—Reprinted. Extra fcap. 8vo. 3s. 6d.
"*There is,*" *the* SATURDAY REVIEW *says,* "*all the old fun, the old sense of social ease and brightness and freedom, the old medley of work and indolence, of jest and earnest, that made Oxford life so picturesque.*"

Palgrave.—Works by FRANCIS TURNER PALGRAVE, M.A., late Fellow of Exeter College, Oxford:—
THE FIVE DAYS' ENTERTAINMENTS AT WENTWORTH GRANGE. A Book for Children. With Illustrations by ARTHUR HUGHES, and Engraved Title-page by JEENS. Small 4to. cloth extra. 6s.
"*If you want a really good book for both sexes and all ages, buy this, as handsome a volume of tales as you'll find in all the market.*"—ATHENÆUM. "*Exquisite both in form and substance.*"—GUARDIAN.
LYRICAL POEMS. Extra fcap. 8vo. 6s.
"*A volume of pure quiet verse, sparkling with tender melodies, and alive with thoughts of genuine poetry.... Turn where we will throughout the volume, we find traces of beauty, tenderness, and truth; true poet's work, touched and refined by the master-hand of a real artist, who shows his genius even in trifles.*"—STANDARD.
ORIGINAL HYMNS. Third Edition, enlarged, 18mo. 1s. 6d.
"*So choice, so perfect, and so refined, so tender in feeling, and so scholarly in expression, that we look with special interest to everything that he gives us.*"—LITERARY CHURCHMAN.
GOLDEN TREASURY OF THE BEST SONGS AND LYRICS. Edited by F. T. PALGRAVE. See GOLDEN TREASURY SERIES.
SHAKESPEARE'S SONNETS AND SONGS. Edited by F. T. PALGRAVE. Gem Edition. With Vignette Title by JEENS. 3s. 6d.
"*For minute elegance no volume could possibly excel the 'Gem Edition.'*"—SCOTSMAN.

Parables.—TWELVE PARABLES OF OUR LORD. Illustrated in Colours from Sketches taken in the East by MCENIRY with Frontispiece from a Picture by JOHN JELLICOE, and Illuminated Texts and Borders. Royal 4to. in Ornamental Binding. 16s.

BELLES LETTRES.

The TIMES *calls it "one of the most beautiful of modern pictorial works;" while the* GRAPHIC *says "nothing in this style, so good, has ever before been published."*

Patmore.—THE CHILDREN'S GARLAND, from the Best Poets. Selected and arranged by COVENTRY PATMORE. New Edition. With Illustrations by J. LAWSON. Crown 8vo. gilt. 6s. Golden Treasury Edition. 18mo. 4s. 6d.

"*The charming illustrations added to many of the poems will add greatly to their value in the eyes of children.*"—DAILY NEWS.

Pember.—THE TRAGEDY OF LESBOS. A Dramatic Poem. By E. H. PEMBER. Fcap. 8vo. 4s. 6d.

Founded upon the story of Sappho. "He tells his story with dramatic force, and in language that often rises almost to grandeur."—ATHENÆUM.

Poole.—PICTURES OF COTTAGE LIFE IN THE WEST OF ENGLAND. By MARGARET E. POOLE. New and Cheaper Edition. With Frontispiece by R. FARREN. Crown 8vo. 3s. 6d.

"*Charming stories of peasant life, written in something of George Eliot's style. . . . Her stories could not be other than they are, as literal as truth, as romantic as fiction, full of pathetic touches and strokes of genuine humour. . . . All the stories are studies of actual life, executed with no mean art.*"—TIMES.

Population of an Old Pear Tree. From the French of F. VAN BRUYSSEL. Edited by the Author of "The Heir of Redclyffe." With Illustrations by BECKER. Cheaper Edition. Crown 8vo. gilt. 4s. 6d.

"*This is not a regular book of natural history, but a description of all the living creatures that came and went in a summer's day beneath an old pear tree, observed by eyes that had for the nonce become microscopic, recorded by a pen that finds dramas in everything, and illustrated by a dainty pencil. . . . We can hardly fancy anyone with a moderate turn for the curiosities of insect life, or for delicate French esprit, not being taken by these clever sketches.*"—GUARDIAN. "*A whimsical and charming little book.*"—ATHENÆUM.

Prince Florestan of Monaco, The Fall of. By HIMSELF. New Edition, with Illustration and Map. 8vo. cloth. Extra gilt edges, 5s. A French Translation, 5s. Also an Edition for the People. Crown 8vo. 1s.

"*Those who have read only the extracts given, will not need to be told how amusing and happily touched it is. Those who read it for other purposes than amusement can hardly miss the sober and sound political lessons with which its light pages abound, and which are as much needed in England as by the nation to whom the author directly addresses his moral.*"—PALL MALL GAZETTE. "*This little book is very clever, wild with animal spirits, but showing plenty of good sense, amid all the heedless nonsense which fills so many of its pages.*"—DAILY NEWS. "*In an age little remarkable for powers of political satire, the sparkle of the pages gives them every claim to welcome.*"—STANDARD.

Rankine.—SONGS AND FABLES. By W. J. McQuorn Rankine, late Professor of Civil Engineering and Mechanics at Glasgow. With Illustrations. Crown 8vo. 6s.
"*A lively volume of verses, full of a fine manly spirit, much humour and geniality. The illustrations are admirably conceived, and executed with fidelity and talent.*"—MORNING POST.

Realmah.—By the Author of "Friends in Council." Crown 8vo. 6s.

Rhoades.—POEMS. By JAMES RHOADES. Fcap. 8vo. 4s. 6d.

Richardson.—THE ILIAD OF THE EAST. A Selection of Legends drawn from Valmiki's Sanskrit Poem, "The Ramayana." By FREDERIKA RICHARDSON. Crown 8vo. 7s. 6d.
"*It is impossible to read it without recognising the value and interest of the Eastern epic. It is as fascinating as a fairy tale, this romantic poem of India.*"—GLOBE. "*A charming volume, which at once enmeshes the reader in its snares.*"—ATHENÆUM.

Roby.—STORY OF A HOUSEHOLD, AND OTHER POEMS. By MARY K. ROBY. Fcap. 8vo. 5s.

Rogers.—Works by J. E. ROGERS:—
RIDICULA REDIVIVA. Old Nursery Rhymes. Illustrated in Colours, with Ornamental Cover. Crown 4to. 3s. 6d.
"*The most splendid, and at the same time the most really meritorious of the books specially intended for children, that we have seen.*"—SPECTATOR. "*These large bright pictures will attract children to really good and honest artistic work, and that ought not to be an indifferent consideration with parents who propose to educate their children.*"—PALL MALL GAZETTE.
MORES RIDICULI. Old Nursery Rhymes. Illustrated in Colours, with Ornamental Cover. Crown 4to. 3s. 6d.
"*These world-old rhymes have never had and need never wish for a better pictorial setting than Mr. Rogers has given them.*"—TIMES. "*Nothing could be quainter or more absurdly comical than most of the pictures, which are all carefully executed and beautifully coloured.*"—GLOBE.

Rossetti.—GOBLIN MARKET, AND OTHER POEMS. By CHRISTINA ROSSETTI. With two Designs by D. G. ROSSETTI. Second Edition. Fcap. 8vo. 5s.
"*She handles her little marvel with that rare poetic discrimination which neither exhausts it of its simple wonders by pushing symbolism too far, nor keeps those wonders in the merely fabulous and capricious stage. In fact, she has produced a true children's poem, which is far more delightful to the mature than to children, though it would be delightful to all.*"—SPECTATOR.

Runaway (The). A Story for the Young. By the Author of "Mrs. Jerningham's Journal." With Illustrations by J. LAWSON. Globe 8vo. gilt. 4s. 6d.
"*This is one of the best, if not indeed the very best, of all the stories that has come before us this Christmas. The heroines are both*

charming, and, unlike heroines, they are as full of fun as of charms. It is an admirable book to read aloud to the young folk when they are all gathered round the fire, and nurses and other apparitions are still far away."—SATURDAY REVIEW.

Ruth and her Friends. A Story for Girls. With a Frontispiece. Fourth Edition. 18mo. Cloth extra. 2s. 6d.

"*We wish all the school girls and home-taught girls in the land had the opportunity of reading it.*"—NONCONFORMIST.

Scouring of the White Horse; or, the Long VACATION RAMBLE OF A LONDON CLERK. Illustrated by DOYLE. Imp. 16mo. Cheaper Issue. 3s. 6d.

"*A glorious tale of summer joy.*"—FREEMAN. "*There is a genial hearty life about the book.*"—JOHN BULL. "*The execution is excellent. . . . Like 'Tom Brown's School Days,' the 'White Horse' gives the reader a feeling of gratitude and personal esteem towards the author.*"—SATURDAY REVIEW.

Shairp (Principal).—KILMAHOE, a Highland Pastoral, with other Poems. By JOHN CAMPBELL SHAIRP, Principal of the United College, St. Andrews. Fcap. 8vo. 5s.

"*Kilmahoe is a Highland Pastoral, redolent of the warm soft air of the western lochs and moors, sketched out with remarkable grace and picturesqueness.*"—SATURDAY REVIEW.

Shakespeare.—The Works of WILLIAM SHAKESPEARE. Cambridge Edition. Edited by W. GEORGE CLARK, M.A. and W. ALDIS WRIGHT, M.A. Nine vols. 8vo. Cloth. 4l. 14s. 6d.

The GUARDIAN *calls it an "excellent, and, to the student, almost indispensable edition ;" and the* EXAMINER *calls it "an unrivalled edition."*

Shakespeare's Tempest. Edited with Glossarial and Explanatory Notes, by the Rev. J. M. JEPHSON. New Edition. 18mo. 1s.

Slip (A) in the Fens.—Illustrated by the Author. Crown 8vo. 6s.

"*An artistic little volume, for every page is a picture.*"—TIMES. "*It will be read with pleasure, and with a pleasure that is altogether innocent.*"—SATURDAY REVIEW.

Smith.—POEMS. By CATHERINE BARNARD SMITH. Fcap. 8vo. 5s.

"*Wealthy in feeling, meaning, finish, and grace; not without passion, which is suppressed, but the keener for that.*"—ATHENÆUM.

Smith (Rev. Walter).—HYMNS OF CHRIST AND THE CHRISTIAN LIFE. By the Rev. WALTER C. SMITH, M.A. Fcap. 8vo. 6s.

"*These are among the sweetest sacred poems we have read for a long time. With no profuse imagery, expressing a range of feeling and expression by no means uncommon, they are true and elevated, and their pathos is profound and simple.*"—NONCONFORMIST.

Spring Songs. By a WEST HIGHLANDER. With a Vignette Illustration by GOURLAY STEELE. Fcap. 8vo. 1s. 6d.
"*Without a trace of affectation or sentimentalism, these utterances are perfectly simple and natural, profoundly human and profoundly true.*"—DAILY NEWS.

Stanley.—TRUE TO LIFE.—A SIMPLE STORY. By MARY STANLEY. Crown 8vo. 10s. 6d.
"*For many a long day we have not met with a more simple, healthy, and unpretending story.*"—STANDARD.

Stephen (C. E.)—THE SERVICE OF THE POOR; being an Inquiry into the Reasons for and against the Establishment of Religious Sisterhoods for Charitable Purposes. By CAROLINE EMILIA STEPHEN. Crown 8vo. 6s. 6d.
"*It touches incidentally and with much wisdom and tenderness on so many of the relations of women, particularly of single women, with society, that it may be read with advantage by many who have never thought of entering a Sisterhood.*"—SPECTATOR.

Stephens (J. B.)—CONVICT ONCE. A Poem. By J. BRUNTON STEPHENS. Extra fcap. 8vo. 3s. 6d.
"*It is as far more interesting than ninety-nine novels out of a hundred, as it is superior to them in power, worth, and beauty. We should most strongly advise everybody to read 'Convict Once.'*"—WESTMINSTER REVIEW.

Streets and Lanes of a City: Being the Reminiscences of AMY DUTTON. With a Preface by the BISHOP OF SALISBURY. Second and Cheaper Edition. Globe 8vo. 2s. 6d.
"*One of the most really striking books that has ever come before us.*"—LITERARY CHURCHMAN.

Thring.—SCHOOL SONGS. A Collection of Songs for Schools. With the Music arranged for four Voices. Edited by the Rev. E. THRING and H. RICCIUS. Folio. 7s. 6d.
The collection includes the "Agnus Dei," Tennyson's "Light Brigade," Macaulay's "Ivry," etc. among other pieces.

Tom Brown's School Days.—By AN OLD BOY. Golden Treasury Edition, 4s. 6d. People's Edition, 2s. With Seven Illustrations by A. HUGHES and SYDNEY HALL. Crown 8vo. 6s.
"*The most famous boy's book in the language.*"—DAILY NEWS.

Tom Brown at Oxford.—New Edition. With Illustrations. Crown 8vo. 6s.
"*In no other work that we can call to mind are the finer qualities of the English gentleman more happily portrayed.*"—DAILY NEWS.
"*A book of great power and truth.*"—NATIONAL REVIEW.

Trench.—Works by R. CHENEVIX TRENCH, D.D., Archbishop of Dublin. (For other Works by this Author, see THEOLOGICAL, HISTORICAL, and PHILOSOPHICAL CATALOGUES.)
POEMS. Collected and arranged anew. Fcap. 8vo. 7s. 6d.

BELLES LETTRES.

Trench (Archbishop)—*continued.*
ELEGIAC POEMS. Third Edition. Fcap. 8vo. 2s. 6d.
CALDERON'S LIFE'S A DREAM: The Great Theatre of the World. With an Essay on his Life and Genius. Fcap. 8vo. 4s. 6d.
HOUSEHOLD BOOK OF ENGLISH POETRY. Selected and arranged, with Notes, by Archbishop TRENCH. Second Edition. Extra fcap. 8vo. 5s. 6d.
"*The Archbishop has conferred in this delightful volume an important gift on the whole English-speaking population of the world.*"—PALL MALL GAZETTE.
SACRED LATIN POETRY, Chiefly Lyrical. Selected and arranged for Use. By Archbishop TRENCH. Third Edition, Corrected and Improved. Fcap. 8vo. 7s.
JUSTIN MARTYR, AND OTHER POEMS. Fifth Edition. Fcap. 8vo. 6s.

Trollope (Anthony).—SIR HARRY HOTSPUR OF HUMBLETHWAITE. By ANTHONY TROLLOPE, Author of "Framley Parsonage," etc. Cheap Edition. Globe 8vo. 2s. 6d.
The ATHENÆUM *remarks:* "*No reader who begins to read this book is likely to lay it down until the last page is turned. This brilliant novel appears to us decidedly more successful than any other of Mr. Trollope's shorter stories.*"

Turner.—Works by the Rev. CHARLES TENNYSON TURNER:—
SONNETS. Dedicated to his Brother, the Poet Laureate. Fcap. 8vo. 4s. 6d.
SMALL TABLEAUX. Fcap. 8vo. 4s. 6d.

Under the Limes.—By the Author of "Christina North." Second Edition. Crown 8vo. 6s.
"*The readers of 'Christina North' are not likely to have forgotten that bright, fresh, picturesque story, nor will they be slow to welcome so pleasant a companion to it as this. It abounds in happy touches of description, of pathos, and insight into the life and passion of true love.*"—STANDARD. "*One of the prettiest and best told stories which it has been our good fortune to read for a long time.*"—PALL MALL GAZETTE.

Vittoria Colonna.—LIFE AND POEMS. By MRS. HENRY ROSCOE. Crown 8vo. 9s.
"*It is written with good taste, with quick and intelligent sympathy, occasionally with a real freshness and charm of style.*"—PALL MALL GAZETTE.

Waller.—SIX WEEKS IN THE SADDLE: A Painter's Journal in Iceland. By S. E. WALLER. Illustrated by the Author. Crown 8vo. 6s.
"*An exceedingly pleasant and naturally written little book. . . . Mr. Waller has a clever pencil, and the text is well illustrated with his own sketches.*"—TIMES.

Wandering Willie. By the Author of "Effie's Friends," and "John Hatherton." Third Edition. Crown 8vo. 6s.

"*This is an idyll of rare truth and beauty. . . . The story is simple and touching, the style of extraordinary delicacy, precision, and picturesqueness. . . . A charming gift-book for young ladies not yet promoted to novels, and will amply repay those of their elders who may give an hour to its perusal.*"—DAILY NEWS.

Webster.—Works by AUGUSTA WEBSTER:—

"*If Mrs. Webster only remains true to herself, she will assuredly take a higher rank as a poet than any woman has yet done.*"—WESTMINSTER REVIEW.

DRAMATIC STUDIES. Extra fcap. 8vo. 5s.
"*A volume as strongly marked by perfect taste as by poetic power.*"—NONCONFORMIST.

A WOMAN SOLD, AND OTHER POEMS. Crown 8vo. 7s. 6d.
"*Mrs. Webster has shown us that she is able to draw admirably from the life; that she can observe with subtlety, and render her observations with delicacy; that she can impersonate complex conceptions and venture into which few living writers can follow her.*"—GUARDIAN.

PORTRAITS. Second Edition. Extra fcap. 8vo. 3s. 6d.
"*Mrs. Webster's poems exhibit simplicity and tenderness . . . her taste is perfect . . . This simplicity is combined with a subtlety of thought, feeling, and observation which demand that attention which only real lovers of poetry are apt to bestow.*"—WESTMINSTER REVIEW.

PROMETHEUS BOUND OF ÆSCHYLUS. Literally translated into English Verse. Extra fcap. 8vo. 3s. 6d.
"*Closeness and simplicity combined with literary skill.*"—ATHENÆUM. "*Mrs. Webster's 'Dramatic Studies' and 'Translation of Prometheus' have won for her an honourable place among our female poets. She writes with remarkable vigour and dramatic realisation, and bids fair to be the most successful claimant of Mrs. Browning's mantle.*"—BRITISH QUARTERLY REVIEW.

MEDEA OF EURIPIDES. Literally translated into English Verse. Extra fcap. 8vo. 3s. 6d.
"*Mrs. Webster's translation surpasses our utmost expectations. It is a photograph of the original without any of that harshness which so often accompanies a photograph.*"—WESTMINSTER REVIEW.

THE AUSPICIOUS DAY. A Dramatic Poem. Extra fcap. 8vo. 5s.
"*The 'Auspicious Day' shows a marked advance, not only in art, but, in what is of far more importance, in breadth of thought and intellectual grasp.*"—WESTMINSTER REVIEW. "*This drama is a manifestation of high dramatic power on the part of the gifted writer, and entitled to our warmest admiration, as a worthy piece of work.*"—STANDARD.

YU-PE-YA'S LUTE. A Chinese Tale in English Verse. Extra fcap. 8vo. 3s. 6d.
"*A very charming tale, charmingly told in dainty verse, with occasional lyrics of tender beauty.*"—STANDARD. "*We close the*

Webster—*continued.*

book with the renewed conviction that in Mrs. Webster we have a profound and original poet. The book is marked not by mere sweetness of melody—rare as that gift is—but by the infinitely rarer gifts of dramatic power, of passion, and sympathetic insight."
—WESTMINSTER REVIEW.

When I was a Little Girl. STORIES FOR CHILDREN. By the Author of "St. Olave's." Fourth Edition. Extra fcap. 8vo. 4s. 6d. With Eight Illustrations by L. FRÖLICH.

"At the head, and a long way ahead, of all books for girls, we place 'When I was a Little Girl.'"—TIMES. "It is one of the choicest morsels of child-biography which we have met with."—NONCONFORMIST.

White.—RHYMES BY WALTER WHITE. 8vo. 7s. 6d.

Whittier.—JOHN GREENLEAF WHITTIER'S POETICAL WORKS. Complete Edition, with Portrait engraved by C. H. JEENS. 18mo. 4s. 6d.

"Mr. Whittier has all the smooth melody and the pathos of the author of 'Hiawatha,' with a greater nicety of description and a quainter fancy."—GRAPHIC.

Wolf.—THE LIFE AND HABITS OF WILD ANIMALS. Twenty Illustrations by JOSEPH WOLF, engraved by J. W. and E. WHYMPER. With descriptive Letter-press, by D. G. ELLIOT, F.L.S. Super royal 4to, cloth extra, gilt edges. 21s.

This is the last series of drawings which will be made by Mr. Wolf, either upon wood or stone. The PALL MALL GAZETTE says: "The fierce, untameable side of brute nature has never received a more robust and vigorous interpretation, and the various incidents in which particular character is shown are set forth with rare dramatic power. For excellence that will endure, we incline to place this very near the top of the list of Christmas books." And the ART JOURNAL observes, "Rarely, if ever, have we seen animal life more forcibly and beautifully depicted than in this really splendid volume."

Also, an Edition in royal folio, handsomely bound in Morocco elegant, Proofs before Letters, each Proof signed by the Engravers. Price 8l. 8s.

Wollaston.—LYRA DEVONIENSIS. By T. V. WOLLASTON, M.A. Fcap. 8vo. 3s. 6d.

"It is the work of a man of refined taste, of deep religious sentiment, a true artist, and a good Christian."—CHURCH TIMES.

Woolner.—MY BEAUTIFUL LADY. By THOMAS WOOLNER. With a Vignette by ARTHUR HUGHES. Third Edition. Fcap. 8vo. 5s.

"No man can read this poem without being struck by the fitness and finish of the workmanship, so to speak, as well as by the chastened and unpretending loftiness of thought which pervades the whole."
—GLOBE.

Words from the Poets. Selected by the Editor of "Rays of Sunlight." With a Vignette and Frontispiece. 18mo. limp., 1s.
"*The selection aims at popularity, and deserves it.*"—GUARDIAN.

Yonge (C. M.)—Works by CHARLOTTE M. YONGE.
THE HEIR OF REDCLYFFE. Twentieth Edition. With Illustrations. Crown 8vo. 6s.
HEARTSEASE. Thirteenth Edition. With Illustrations. Crown 8vo. 6s.
THE DAISY CHAIN. Twelfth Edition. With Illustrations. Crown 8vo. 6s.
THE TRIAL: MORE LINKS OF THE DAISY CHAIN. Twelfth Edition. With Illustrations. Crown 8vo. 6s.
DYNEVOR TERRACE. Sixth Edition. Crown 8vo. 6s.
HOPES AND FEARS. Fourth Edition. Crown 8vo. 6s.
THE YOUNG STEPMOTHER. Fifth Edition. Crown 8vo. 6s.
CLEVER WOMAN OF THE FAMILY. Third Edition. Crown 8vo. 6s.
THE DOVE IN THE EAGLE'S NEST. Fourth Edition. Crown 8vo. 6s.
"*We think the authoress of 'The Heir of Redclyffe' has surpassed her previous efforts in this illuminated chronicle of the olden time.*"—BRITISH QUARTERLY.
THE CAGED LION. Illustrated. Third Edition. Crown 8vo. 6s.
"*Prettily and tenderly written, and will with young people especially be a great favourite.*"—DAILY NEWS. "*Everybody should read this.*"—LITERARY CHURCHMAN.
THE CHAPLET OF PEARLS; OR, THE WHITE AND BLACK RIBAUMONT. Crown 8vo. 6s. New Edition.
"*Miss Yonge has brought a lofty aim as well as high art to the construction of a story which may claim a place among the best efforts in historical romance.*"—MORNING POST. "*The plot, in truth, is of the very first order of merit.*"—SPECTATOR. "*We have seldom read a more charming story.*"—GUARDIAN.
THE PRINCE AND THE PAGE. A Tale of the Last Crusade. Illustrated. 18mo. 2s. 6d.
"*A tale which, we are sure, will give pleasure to many others besides the young people for whom it is specially intended. ... This extremely prettily-told story does not require the guarantee afforded by the name of the author of 'The Heir of Redclyffe' on the title-page to ensure its becoming a universal favourite.*"—DUBLIN EVENING MAIL.
THE LANCES OF LYNWOOD. New Edition, with Coloured Illustrations. 18mo. 4s. 6d.
"*The illustrations are very spirited and rich in colour, and the story can hardly fail to charm the youthful reader.*"—MANCHESTER EXAMINER.
THE LITTLE DUKE: RICHARD THE FEARLESS. New Edition. Illustrated. 18mo. 2s. 6d.

Yonge (C. M.)—*continued*.

A STOREHOUSE OF STORIES. First and Second Series. Globe 8vo. 3*s*. 6*d*. each.

CONTENTS OF FIRST SERIES:—History of Philip Quarll—Goody Twoshoes—The Governess—Jemima Placid—The Perambulations of a Mouse—The Village School—The Little Queen—History of Little Jack.

"*Miss Yonge has done great service to the infantry of this generation by putting these eleven stories of sage simplicity within their reach.*"—BRITISH QUARTERLY REVIEW.

CONTENTS OF SECOND SERIES:—Family Stories—Elements of Morality—A Puzzle for a Curious Girl—Blossoms of Morality.

A BOOK OF GOLDEN DEEDS OF ALL TIMES AND ALL COUNTRIES. Gathered and Narrated Anew. New Edition, with Twenty Illustrations by FRÖLICH. Crown 8vo. cloth gilt. 6*s*. (See also GOLDEN TREASURY SERIES). Cheap Edition. 1*s*.

"*We have seen no prettier gift-book for a long time, and none which, both for its cheapness and the spirit in which it has been compiled, is more deserving of praise.*"—ATHENÆUM.

LITTLE LUCY'S WONDERFUL GLOBE. Pictured by FRÖLICH, and narrated by CHARLOTTE M. YONGE. Second Edition. Crown 4to. cloth gilt. 6*s*.

"'*Lucy's Wonderful Globe' is capital, and will give its youthful readers more idea of foreign countries and customs than any number of books of geography or travel.*"—GRAPHIC.

CAMEOS FROM ENGLISH HISTORY. From ROLLO to EDWARD II. Extra fcap. 8vo. 5*s*. Second Edition, enlarged. 5*s*.

A SECOND SERIES. THE WARS IN FRANCE. Extra fcap. 8vo. 5*s*.

"*Instead of dry details,*" says the NONCONFORMIST, "*we have living pictures, faithful, vivid, and striking.*"

P's AND Q's; OR, THE QUESTION OF PUTTING UPON. With Illustrations by C. O. MURRAY. Second Edition. Globe 8vo. cloth gilt. 4*s*. 6*d*.

"*One of her most successful little pieces . . . . just what a narrative should be, each incident simply and naturally related, no preaching or moralising, and yet the moral coming out most powerfully, and the whole story not too long, or with the least appearance of being spun out.*"—LITERARY CHURCHMAN.

THE PILLARS OF THE HOUSE; OR, UNDER WODE, UNDER RODE. Second Edition. Four vols. crown 8vo. 20*s*.

"*A domestic story of English professional life, which for sweetness of tone and absorbing interest from first to last has never been rivalled.*"—STANDARD. "*Miss Yonge has certainly added to her already high reputation by this charming book, which, although in four volumes, is not a single page too long, but keeps the reader's attention fixed to the end. Indeed we are only sorry there is not another volume to come, and part with the Underwood family with sincere regret.*"—COURT CIRCULAR.

Yonge (C. M.)—*continued.*

LADY HESTER; OR, URSULA'S NARRATIVE. Second Edition. Crown 8vo. 6s.

"*We shall not anticipate the interest by epitomizing the plot, but we shall only say that readers will find in it all the gracefulness, right feeling, and delicate perception which they have been long accustomed to look for in Miss Yonge's writings.*"—GUARDIAN.

MACMILLAN'S GOLDEN TREASURY SERIES.

UNIFORMLY printed in 18mo., with Vignette Titles by Sir NOEL PATON, T. WOOLNER, W. HOLMAN HUNT, J. E. MILLAIS, ARTHUR HUGHES, &c. Engraved on Steel by JEENS. Bound in extra cloth, 4s. 6d. each volume. Also kept in morocco and calf bindings.

"*Messrs. Macmillan have, in their Golden Treasury Series, especially provided editions of standard works, volumes of selected poetry, and original compositions, which entitle this series to be called classical. Nothing can be better than the literary execution, nothing more elegant than the material workmanship.*"—BRITISH QUARTERLY REVIEW.

The Golden Treasury of the Best Songs and LYRICAL POEMS IN THE ENGLISH LANGUAGE. Selected and arranged, with Notes, by FRANCIS TURNER PALGRAVE.

"*This delightful little volume, the Golden Treasury, which contains many of the best original lyrical pieces and songs in our language, grouped with care and skill, so as to illustrate each other like the pictures in a well-arranged gallery.*"—QUARTERLY REVIEW.

The Children's Garland from the best Poets. Selected and arranged by COVENTRY PATMORE.

"*It includes specimens of all the great masters in the art of poetry, selected with the matured judgment of a man concentrated on obtaining insight into the feelings and tastes of childhood, and desirous to awaken its finest impulses, to cultivate its keenest sensibilities.*"—MORNING POST.

The Book of Praise. From the Best English Hymn Writers. Selected and arranged by LORD SELBOURNE. *A New and Enlarged Edition.*

"*All previous compilations of this kind must undeniably for the present give place to the Book of Praise. . . . The selection has been made throughout with sound judgment and critical taste. The pains involved in this compilation must have been immense, embracing, as it does, every writer of note in this special province of English literature, and ranging over the most widely divergent tracks of religious thought.*"—SATURDAY REVIEW.

The Fairy Book; the Best Popular Fairy Stories. Selected and rendered anew by the Author of "JOHN HALIFAX, GENTLEMAN."
"*A delightful selection, in a delightful external form; full of the physical splendour and vast opulence of proper fairy tales.*"—SPECTATOR.

The Ballad Book. A Selection of the Choicest British Ballads. Edited by WILLIAM ALLINGHAM.
"*His taste as a judge of old poetry will be found, by all acquainted with the various readings of old English ballads, true enough to justify his undertaking so critical a task.*"—SATURDAY REVIEW.

The Jest Book. The Choicest Anecdotes and Sayings. Selected and arranged by MARK LEMON.
"*The fullest and best jest book that has yet appeared.*"—SATURDAY REVIEW.

Bacon's Essays and Colours of Good and Evil. With Notes and Glossarial Index. By W. ALDIS WRIGHT, M.A.
"*The beautiful little edition of Bacon's Essays, now before us, does credit to the taste and scholarship of Mr. Aldis Wright. . . . It puts the reader in possession of all the essential literary facts and chronology necessary for reading the Essays in connection with Bacon's life and times.*"—SPECTATOR.

The Pilgrim's Progress from this World to that which is to come. By JOHN BUNYAN.
"*A beautiful and scholarly reprint.*"—SPECTATOR.

The Sunday Book of Poetry for the Young. Selected and arranged by C. F. ALEXANDER.
"*A well-selected volume of Sacred Poetry.*"—SPECTATOR.

A Book of Golden Deeds of All Times and All Countries. Gathered and narrated anew. By the Author of "THE HEIR OF REDCLYFFE."
"*. . . To the young, for whom it is especially intended, as a most interesting collection of thrilling tales well told; and to their elders, as a useful handbook of reference, and a pleasant one to take up when their wish is to while away a weary half-hour. We have seen no prettier gift-book for a long time.*"—ATHENÆUM.

The Poetical Works of Robert Burns. Edited, with Biographical Memoir, Notes, and Glossary, by ALEXANDER SMITH. Two Vols.
"*Beyond all question this is the most beautiful edition of Burns yet out.*"—EDINBURGH DAILY REVIEW.

The Adventures of Robinson Crusoe. Edited from the Original Edition by J. W. CLARK, M.A. Fellow of Trinity College, Cambridge.
"*Mutilated and modified editions of this English classic are so much*

the rule, that a cheap and pretty copy of it, rigidly exact to the original, will be a prize to many book-buyers."—EXAMINER.

The Republic of Plato. TRANSLATED into ENGLISH, with Notes by J. LL. DAVIES, M.A. and D. J. VAUGHAN, M.A.
"*A dainty and cheap little edition.*"—EXAMINER.

The Song Book. Words and Tunes from the best Poets and Musicians. Selected and arranged by JOHN HULLAH, Professor of Vocal Music in King's College, London.
"*A choice collection of the sterling songs of England, Scotland, and Ireland, with the music of each prefixed to the Words. How much true wholesome pleasure such a book can diffuse, and will diffuse, we trust through many thousand families.*"—EXAMINER.

La Lyre Française. Selected and arranged, with Notes, by GUSTAVE MASSON, French Master in Harrow School.
A selection of the best French songs and lyrical pieces.

Tom Brown's School Days. By AN OLD BOY.
"*A perfect gem of a book. The best and most healthy book about boys for boys that ever was written.*"—ILLUSTRATED TIMES.

A Book of Worthies. Gathered from the Old Histories and written anew by the Author of "THE HEIR OF REDCLYFFE." With Vignette.
"*An admirable addition to an admirable series.*"—WESTMINSTER REVIEW.

A Book of Golden Thoughts. By HENRY ATTWELL, Knight of the Order of the Oak Crown.
"*Mr. Attwell has produced a book of rare value . . . Happily it is small enough to be carried about in the pocket, and of such a companion it would be difficult to weary.*"—PALL MALL GAZETTE.

Guesses at Truth. By TWO BROTHERS. New Edition.

The Cavalier and his Lady. Selections from the Works of the First Duke and Duchess of Newcastle. With an Introductory Essay by EDWARD JENKINS, Author of "Ginx's Baby," &c. 18mo. 4s. 6d.
"*A charming little volume.*"—STANDARD.

Theologia Germanica.—Which setteth forth many fair Lineaments of Divine Truth, and saith very lofty and lovely things touching a Perfect Life. Edited by DR. PFEIFFER, from the only complete manuscript yet known. Translated from the German, by SUSANNA WINKWORTH. With a Preface by the REV. CHARLES KINGSLEY, and a Letter to the Translator by the Chevalier Bunsen, D.D.

Milton's Poetical Works.—Edited, with Notes, &c., by PROFESSOR MASSON. Two vols. 18mo. 9s.

Scottish Song. A Selection of the Choicest Lyrics of Scotland. Compiled and arranged, with brief Notes, by MARY CARLYLE AITKIN. 18mo. 4s. 6d.

"Miss Aitken's exquisite collection of Scottish Song is so alluring, and suggests so many topics, that we find it difficult to lay it down. The book is one that should find a place in every library, we had almost said in every pocket, and the summer tourist who wishes to carry with him into the country a volume of genuine poetry, will find it difficult to select one containing within so small a compass so much of rarest value."—SPECTATOR.

MACMILLAN'S GLOBE LIBRARY.

Beautifully printed on toned paper and bound in cloth extra, gilt edges, price 4s. 6d. each; in cloth plain, 3s. 6d. Also kept in a variety of calf and morocco bindings at moderate prices.

BOOKS, Wordsworth says, are

"the spirit breathed
By dead men to their kind;"

and the aim of the publishers of the Globe Library has been to make it possible for the universal kin of English-speaking men to hold communion with the loftiest "spirits of the mighty dead;" to put within the reach of all classes *complete* and *accurate* editions, carefully and clearly printed upon the best paper, in a convenient form, at a moderate price, of the works of the MASTER-MINDS OF ENGLISH LITERATURE, and occasionally of foreign literature in an attractive English dress.

The Editors, by their scholarship and special study of their authors, are competent to afford every assistance to readers of all kinds: this assistance is rendered by original biographies, glossaries of unusual or obsolete words, and critical and explanatory notes.

The publishers hope, therefore, that these Globe Editions may prove worthy of acceptance by all classes wherever the English Language is spoken, and by their universal circulation justify their distinctive epithet; while at the same time they spread and nourish a common sympathy with nature's most "finely touched" spirits, and thus help a little to "make the whole world kin."

The SATURDAY REVIEW *says:* "*The Globe Editions are admirable for their scholarly editing, their typographical excellence, their compendious form, and their cheapness.*" *The* BRITISH QUARTERLY REVIEW *says:* "*In compendiousness, elegance, and scholarliness, the Globe Editions of Messrs. Macmillan surpass any popular series* of our classics hitherto given to the public. As near an approach to miniature perfection as has ever been made."

Shakespeare's Complete Works. Edited by W. G. CLARK, M.A., and W. ALDIS WRIGHT, M.A., of Trinity College, Cambridge, Editors of the "Cambridge Shakespeare." With Glossary. pp. 1,075.

The ATHENÆUM *says this edition is "a marvel of beauty, cheapness, and compactness. . . . For the busy man, above all for the working student, this is the best of all existing Shakespeares." And the* PALL MALL GAZETTE *observes: "To have produced the complete works of the world's greatest poet in such a form, and at a price within the reach of every one, is of itself almost sufficient to give the publishers a claim to be considered public benefactors."*

Spenser's Complete Works. Edited from the Original Editions and Manuscripts, by R. MORRIS, with a Memoir by J. W. HALES, M.A. With Glossary. pp. lv, 736.

"Worthy—and higher praise it needs not—of the beautiful 'Globe Series.' The work is edited with all the care so noble a poet deserves."—DAILY NEWS.

Sir Walter Scott's Poetical Works. Edited with a Biographical and Critical Memoir by FRANCIS TURNER PALGRAVE, and copious Notes. pp. xliii, 559.

"We can almost sympathise with a middle-aged grumbler, who, after reading Mr. Palgrave's memoir and introduction, should exclaim—'Why was there not such an edition of Scott when I was a schoolboy?'"—GUARDIAN.

Complete Works of Robert Burns.—THE POEMS, SONGS, AND LETTERS, edited from the best Printed and Manuscript Authorities, with Glossarial Index, Notes, and a Biographical Memoir by ALEXANDER SMITH. pp. lxii, 636. *"Admirable in all respects."*—SPECTATOR. *"The cheapest, the most perfect, and the most interesting edition which has ever been published."*—BELL'S MESSENGER.

Robinson Crusoe. Edited after the Original Editions, with a Biographical Introduction by HENRY KINGSLEY. pp. xxxi, 607. *"A most excellent and in every way desirable edition."*—COURT CIRCULAR. *"Macmillan's 'Globe' Robinson Crusoe is a book to have and to keep."*—MORNING STAR.

Goldsmith's Miscellaneous Works. Edited, with Biographical Introduction, by Professor MASSON. pp. lx, 695. *"Such an admirable compendium of the facts of Goldsmith's life, and so careful and minute a delineation of the mixed traits of his peculiar character as to be a very model of a literary biography in little."*—SCOTSMAN.

Pope's Poetical Works. Edited, with Notes and Introductory Memoir, by ADOLPHUS WILLIAM WARD, M.A., Fellow of St. Peter's College, Cambridge, and Professor of History in Owens College, Manchester. pp. lii, 508.

The LITERARY CHURCHMAN *remarks: " The editor's own notes and introductory memoir are excellent, the memoir alone would be cheap and well worth buying at the price of the whole volume."*

Dryden's Poetical Works. Edited, with a Memoir, Revised Text, and Notes, by W. D. CHRISTIE, M.A., of Trinity College, Cambridge. pp. lxxxvii., 662.

"An admirable edition, the result of great research and of a careful revision of the text. The memoir prefixed contains, within less than ninety pages, as much sound criticism and as comprehensive a biography as the student of Dryden need desire."—PALL MALL GAZETTE.

Cowper's Poetical Works. Edited, with Notes and Biographical Introduction, by WILLIAM BENHAM, Vicar of Addington and Professor of Modern History in Queen's College, London. pp. lxxiii., 536.

"Mr. Benham's edition of Cowper is one of permanent value. The biographical introduction is excellent, full of information, singularly neat and readable and modest—indeed too modest in its comments. The notes are concise and accurate, and the editor has been able to discover and introduce some hitherto unprinted matter. Altogether the book is a very excellent one."—SATURDAY REVIEW.

Morte d'Arthur.—SIR THOMAS MALORY'S BOOK OF KING ARTHUR AND OF HIS NOBLE KNIGHTS OF THE ROUND TABLE. The original Edition of CAXTON, revised for Modern Use. With an Introduction by Sir EDWARD STRACHEY, Bart. pp. xxxvii., 509.

"It is with perfect confidence that we recommend this edition of the old romance to every class of readers."—PALL MALL GAZETTE.

The Works of Virgil. Rendered into English Prose, with Introductions, Notes, Running Analysis, and an Index. By JAMES LONSDALE, M.A., late Fellow and Tutor of Balliol College, Oxford, and Classical Professor in King's College, London; and SAMUEL LEE, M.A., Latin Lecturer at University College, London. pp. 288.

"A more complete edition of Virgil in English it is scarcely possible to conceive than the scholarly work before us."—GLOBE.

The Works of Horace. Rendered into English Prose, with Introductions, Running Analysis, Notes, and Index. By JOHN LONSDALE, M.A., and SAMUEL LEE, M.A.

The STANDARD *says, " To classical and non-classical readers it will be invaluable as a faithful interpretation of the mind and meaning of the poet, enriched as it is with notes and dissertations of the highest value in the way of criticism, illustration, and explanation."*

LONDON: R. CLAY, SONS, AND TAYLOR, PRINTERS.

www.ingramcontent.com/pod-product-compliance
Lightning Source LLC
Chambersburg PA
CBHW022131160426
43197CB00009B/1229